LEADERSHIP EXCELLENCE

LEADERSHIP EXCELLENCE

Dr. R. H. G. Rau

First Edition: 2010

Himalaya Publishing House

MUMBAI • NEW DELHI • NAGPUR • BENGALURU • HYDERABAD • CHENNAI • PUNE • LUCKNOW • AHMEDABAD • ERNAKULAM • BHUBANESWAR • INDORE

First Edition : 2010

Published by : Mrs. Meena Pandey for **Himalaya Publishing House Pvt. Ltd.,**
"Ramdoot", Dr. Bhalerao Marg, Girgaon, **Mumbai - 400 004.**
Phone: 2386 01 70/2386 38 63, Fax: 022-2387 71 78
Email: himpub@vsnl.com Website: www.himpub.com

Branch Offices

New Delhi : "Pooja Apartments", 4-B, Murari Lal Street, Ansari Road, Darya Ganj,
New Delhi - 110 002. Phone:23270392, 23278631 Fax: 011-23256286

Nagpur : Kundanlal Chandak Industrial Estate, Ghat Road, **Nagpur - 440 018.**
Phone: 2738731, 3296733 Telefax : 0712-2721215

Bengaluru : No. 16/1 (Old 12/1), 1st Floor, Next to Hotel Highlands, Madhava Nagar,
Race Course Road, **Bengaluru - 560 001.**
Phone : 22281541, 22385461, Telefax: 080-22286611

Hyderabad : No. 3-4-184, Lingampally, Besides Raghavendra Swamy Matham,Kachiguda,
Hyderabad - 500 027. Phone: 040-27560041, 27550139, Mobile:- 09848130433

Chennai : No. 85/50, Bazullah Road, T. Nagar, **Chennai - 600 017.**
Phone: 044-28144004/28144005

Pune : First Floor, "Laksha" Apartment, No. 527, Mehunpura,
Shaniwarpeth (Near Prabhat Theatre), **Pune - 411 030.**
Phone: 020-24496323/24496333

Lucknow : C-43, Sector - C, Ali Gunj, **Lucknow - 226 024.**
Phone: 0522-2339329

Ahmedabad : 114, "SHAIL", 1st Floor, Opp. Madhu Sudan House, C.G.Road,
Navrang Pura, **Ahmedabad– 380 009.**
Phone: 079-26560126, Mobiles:- 09327324149,09314679413

Ernakulam : 39/104 A, Lakshmi Apartment, Karikkamuri Cross Rd.,
Ernakulam, **Cochin – 622011**, Kerala.
Phone: 0484-2378012, 2378016, Mob.: 09344199799

Bhubaneswar : 5 Station Square, **Bhubaneswar (Orissa) - 751 001.**
Mobile:- 9861046007, E-mail:- orissa@himpub.com

Indore : Kesardeep Avenue Extension, 73, Narayan Bagh, Flat No. 302,
IIIrd Floor, Near Humpty Dumpty School, Narayan Bagh, **Indore 452 007(M.P.)**.
Mobile:- 09301386468

DTP by : HPH, Editorial Office, Bhandup (Deepali)

Printed by : Prabhat Book Binder, Mumbai.

To my beloved mother whose personal and family values made profound impact on my attitude and ability.

PREFACE

For the past four decades, I have been working on various management positions, including manufacturing, service, marketing, quality, research and technology. My professional activity included consultancy to several individuals and organizations in promoting quality values and handholding them towards excellent results. I have also been fortunate in interacting with many leading organizations and outstanding individuals.

This highly enriching experience gave me an insight into the diversity of management styles employed and their effectiveness. Some of them are extremely successful, some also rans, and yet a few laggards.

Leading companies and individuals continue to work with passion and tremendous zeal to continually improve performance. They recognize that there is no finishing line for excellence, and it can come about only through support and participation of all stakeholders. In the Olympics too, records are continuously bettered in each succeeding event, evidently the result of team effort. The same is true of other competing fields.

What is it that separates performers from laggards? It is clearly the application of planned initiatives with sharply focused commitment and its impact on organizational performance. Leading performers have stretched goals and targets, and worked tirelessly towards achieving them in every activity and functional area.

However, it is the focus on 'stretching the stretch' that drives one to passionately work towards sustained leadership position. Pitfalls, if any, are attributable to slippages in implementation rather than lack of passion to lead.

My personal experiences over the years and critical studies of various performances, published or otherwise, are distilled, covered and grouped under seven steps: from Clarity of Purpose to Commitment to Outperform.

This book is written with an objective to provide an insight into this knowledge to help readers strive effectively for outstanding performances.

Dr. R. H. G. Rau

ACKNOWLEDGEMENT

My professional learning process began in 1963 when I joined Mukand Steel, a highly respected and leading steel maker in India. My first lesson on performance was drawn through tremendous admiration at the way Mr. Viren Shah was managing Mukand as its CEO. I am always indebted to him for the early learnings.

The four decades since then broadened my vision through interaction with several global performers, made possible through innumerable trips across the globe. I recall them with gratitude, though I admit that it is a herculean task to list all those influencing leaders.

While Mukand was my launching pad, it was the last nine-year stint at RPG Enterprises that matured my ability as a performance facilitator. I owe a special debt to Mr. Harsh Goenka, RPG Enterprises Chairman, for making this happen.

I would like to thank my wife Vijaya and my daughter Sasi for their assistance in drafting and editing. Special thanks are due to Himalaya Publishing House for printing and publishing this book.

Dr. R. H. G. Rau

CONTENTS

1 Chapter

KEEP YOUR PURPOSE CLEAR

Leadership performances are consistently conspicuous when they are value-driven

CONTENTS:

1.1 DRILL DOWN VALUES

Ensure that efforts for excellent performances are in line with basic policy statements such as the organization's vision, mission and support policy statements, including quality policy.

APPRECIATION

Many outstanding organizations have **established** principles based on the convictions of their senior management. These principles provide direction to structurally evolve organizational values and spread them across every function. Managerial strategies are a derivative of these values and the deployed strategies are a reflection of these principles.

When successfully deployed, strategies provide a guideline for setting both long-term and short-term objectives. The guiding principles invariably help employees to direct their efforts towards excellent performances.

The other day, I visited Barnes and Noble, the leading booksellers in the USA. I was at the stores located on the Stevens Creek, San Jose, which has a remarkable array of books, audios and videos catering to a wide readership.

I walked into the men's rest room and was amused to see an instruction prominently displayed, "Employees must wash hands before returning to work". Such an instruction is usually practised by some of the leading retail eateries in the country.

Out of curiosity, I asked one of the employees what prompted the management to issue the instruction, and the answer was because they immensely "value" their books. Any employee who is found showing any disrespect to this rule is booted out the next moment. Such is the power of conviction.

Among the different value statements evolved, Vision and Mission Statements are the most common. Vision Statements are relatively more abstract and reflect the management's dream to achieve something big for the organization.

All visionaries dream – not daydream. They are fully conscious of the organization's existing competence level and desire to take it to greater heights. Invariably, there is a huge gap to be filled, which is a challenge to achieving the **current unachievable over a period of time.**

Being philosophical by nature and of abstract content, vision statements are often the subject of ridicule. It is only a visionary who will not only dream big but also doggedly work to get his dream fulfilled. Perseverance is the key attribute of any visionary. A vision is, thus, a dream put into action.

Creating a vision statement for an organization is often a complex task, requiring some artistry because visions often evolve without great detail. Vision statements need not be lengthy but must be powerful, containing basically three elements.

First, it must have direction; second, it must help in the evolution of measurable objectives with metrics; and third, **it must have the ability to stretch performance.** In fact, a vision is "Changing to Outperform". A vision statement is the fundamental way the company management communicates across the organization.

Leaders are not ashamed of dreaming. Indeed they love to do it. They do it continuously, openly and passionately sharing their aspirations with others. Outstanding performers systematically and ruthlessly work towards achieving their dreams. The achievement of desired results establishes much credibility, enough to make others envious.

In comparison, Mission Statements are short-term by nature and are managed with specifics achievable overtime. To that extent, these statements are less abstract. They have quantifiable and measurable targets with definite timeframes. The targets are well-defined and reflect the set organizational and personal goals. They are related to the current set of activities and do not exhibit any vagueness.

For those organizations having both vision and mission statements, the latter is not a standalone. It is necessarily aligned to the declared vision statement.

Vision and mission statements, as Basic Policy Statements, are evolved through consultation and consensus, but directed by the senior management. Further, they are built around expressions of core values that reflect the committed principles of the organization.

Leaders proactively manage their vision and mission. The management process includes passion to achieve these basic policy statements without compromising on the declared values.

Organizations periodically revisit the evolved value statements to ensure their validity and whether they have withstood the test of time, while quickly initiating course corrections wherever required.

Management of the basic policy statements needs appropriate support from several other policy statements such as quality policy, human resource policy and environment policy. Evolution of these Support Policies needs wider consultation within the organization and also competency to withstand the rigour of both internal and external system audits and assessments for their strict compliance.

At operating levels, the management achieves the desired results relevant to these value statements by setting annual goals and target-oriented objectives.

Policy statements will be merely decorative if they are not honestly implemented, periodically reviewed and appropriately corrected. Leading organizations commit dynamic reviews for their effective implementation with inspiration and motivation, and work towards continual breakthrough improvements.

APPLICATION

Jamsetji Nusserwanji Tata gave India its first steel plant. That steel plant gave birth to industrial India. Even today, every Indian proudly acknowledges this singular achievement.

Jamsetji was 43 when, in 1882, he first read a report by a German geologist that the iron ore deposits in Chanda, Maharashtra were the best **in the world**. Deposits of coal, the other major raw material for steel making, were also located nearby.

Jamsetji envisaged his mission of the first steel mill in India, for he also had a vision of India producing its own steel for industrial progress.

Since test facilities in India were limited, Jamsetji took the samples of the coal to Germany for testing. The coal was declared unsuitable for steel making. He wanted to pursue the matter but, having learnt that the mining terms offered by the British Government were too restrictive, he gave up the project.

But, he did not give up the mission.

For the next seventeen years, Jamsetji kept a record of clippings on minerals available in India and their characteristics. When mining terms were liberalized in 1899, Jamsetji took up the project once again. He was then 60.

He met several government officials in England, studied the steel making process himself at Alabama, USA, visited the world's largest iron-ore market in Cleveland, USA and met metallurgists, geologists and engineers across the globe.

A geologist arrived in India in 1903. He studied the Chanda project but gave up on it and was ready to return home. Jamsetji's mission, focus and commitment urged the expert to stay on and look for another location.

The efforts continued. Braving the Indian sun, Indian jungles, elephants and tigers, and uncomfortable modes of transport which included travelling in a bullock cart, the plant location was finalised. Later, the Tatas had to face an uncooperative financial world. And they did.

Jamsetji died in 1904. The mission continued. The first ingot rolled out from the Jamshedpur steel plant in February 1912. It marked the birth of industrial India.

An outstanding example of a visionary approach implemented with missionary zeal.

KEY LEARNING

Value statements are not decorative posters.

1.2 FOCUS ON EVERY ACTION

Focus, focus, focus. Do not digress or deviate.

APPRECIATION

Do we see blurred managements around us? It is disturbing that over eighty per cent of Indian organizations researched are blurred, resulting in most of their efforts getting dissipated. They are unproductive negative, discouraging and expensive.

Such malaise is due to a combination of confusing concepts, practices that are convenient, and frequent shifts in objectives. They are so widespread and embedded so deep into the organizational culture, they often get justified as "routine". Surprisingly, several respondents studied said that it was a "part and parcel" of their operations and can be rid off only through a managerial surgery. That is the reason why very few leaders' names are known among the leading Indian organizations.

Blurred concepts are the result of honest anxiety to lead albeit with prevailing confusion on the approaches that should be adopted. Concepts are invariably borrowed from those who had successfully adopted them, with a belief that they should work with them too.

Potentially successful concepts are generalised ideas having a strong relationship with a level of understanding and a commitment for implementation. Just like ideas, concepts also need to be nurtured, and be relevant and meaningful to the specific organizational goals.

Most managements are impressed with new concepts and attempt to implement them without any honest and objective scrutiny, or even the basic understanding of these concepts. Such an approach is bound to lead to disappointment. Even though the organization decides to work on well understood concepts and a set of generalised ideas, they must make fair efforts at implementation.

Many organizations suffer from the "Practice the Convenient" syndrome. They believe that any practice that can be easily understood and deployed is good and have high comfort levels in maintaining current practices. There is considerable resistance for adaptation of any new practice. Efforts are often conspicuous to convince one and all as to why new practices cannot be implemented or are even harmful to the organization.

There is nothing like a permanent great practice. Relevance of any good practice falls flat over a period of time. One must never neglect the importance of the time element.

When a statement of objectives and setting of targets are not given the seriousness they deserve, quite a few managers easily dodge their responsibilities. Accountability will then be the casualty. CEOs often express their concern in formal meetings like, "I do not want to hear any complaints from any of my customers". Such statements are hollow and mean nothing. Everyone would listen and soon forget about them. Complaints continue to pour in and will be reviewed all over again in many subsequent meetings.

Such drifts are some of the prime reasons why management efforts do not obtain desired results. They are conspicuous to anyone who cares to look deeply at the obvious. It does not require any great effort. They are evident right from the setting of goals to the organizational behaviour and performance, to later activities including reviews for both achievements and slippages.

The only way such drifts can be arrested is focusing with tremendous clarity on each step of the process. The sharper the focus, the better the results. Every step in management therefore demands that all those involved at every process have a common understanding of what is being sought.

Further, each member of the organization should be trained on how to focus on important issues and avoid drifting during implementation. Inputs such as institutionalised quantification and facilitation ensure that all management initiatives have definite focus.

APPLICATION

"Come on boys, we will play a game," said Dr. V. B. Joshi, in his own exuberant style.

As Head of the Research Centre at Mukand Iron & Steel Works Ltd., Bombay, Joshi was well known for his unconventional ways of entertaining and motivating his staff. Being a leading steel and iron foundry in India, way back in the early 1960s, Mukand's management was extremely impressed with the research and development work conducted by leading organizations like Steel Casting Research and Trade Association (SCRATA) in the U.S.A. and British Iron and Steel Research Association (BISRA), and decided to create an inhouse research facility comparable to global standards. Joshi, then teaching at Indian Institute of Technology, Bombay, was chosen to lead the company's R&D team.

Joshi quickly put in place a five-member team of young, energetic and dedicated scientists and engineers: three of them science doctorates and two holding bachelor degrees in engineering. By the time Mukand's Research Centre celebrated its first anniversary, the team had several new developments to its credit. The company was highly appreciative of the quality of their work and some of the research findings were beyond the expectations of the management and the industry.

Joshi was so unconventional in his approach, he used to spend several hours just chatting with colleagues around, visibly doing nothing. But, his every single intervention had a purpose that became apparent only after a period of time.

When Joshi called the boys for the game, all five members of his staff joined him outside the research building. After putting them at ease, suddenly Joshi said, "I want you to run a race and collect the winner's prize!"

The boys quickly cleared their tables and gathered around him, eager to participate in the race. But the rules of the race were somewhat unusual. Joshi said, "I will be at the finishing point at a distance, under that mango tree, and you must reach me. But the winner is not the one who runs the fastest but the one who runs the straightest! I will signal to start the race, start clocking and you must run straight to reach me to win."

So, Joshi went up to a distant point and gave the signal: "Ready! Get set! Go!"

All the five started the run. The first one, while taking his steps, was figuring out how to run straight. The second one appeared to have forgotten that he was in the race, but was more intent at looking at how the other four were running. The third one kept looking at his feet to make sure he was running straight. The fourth one was looking alternately at his right and left sides to align himself on a straight-line. But the fifth one did not look here nor there. His eyes were on his boss who stood at a distance and he ran straight to reach him.

The fifth one, the youngest among the team, was the winner for running straightest. At the same time, he was the fastest. How did he do it? He had his eyes fixed on his goal.

A few months later, when Joshi was scheduled to proceed on a 3-month study tour to the research organizations in Europe and in the U.S.A, it was this youngest boy who was assigned the task of supervising the R&D work of Mukand.

KEY LEARNING

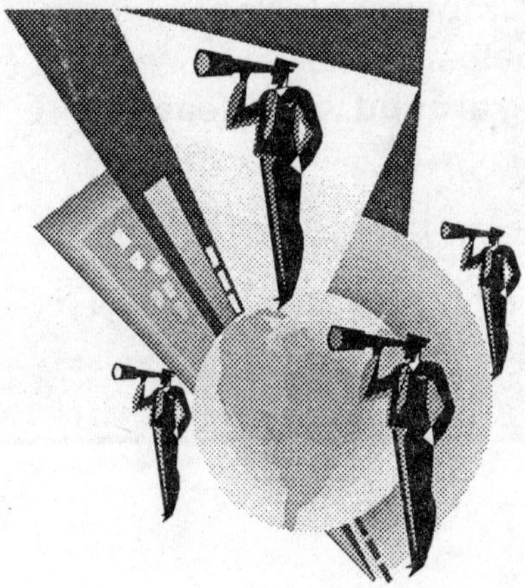

Once focussed, processes get directed and the results are certain.

1.3 PUT IDEAS INTO PRACTICE

Ideas are for implementation.
Facilitation helps.
Avoid floating around with ideas.

APPRECIATION

Ideas are conceptualised thoughts. When expressed in line with specific requirements of a situation, they are extremely important and useful. One can always find a large number of ideas getting generated in any management discussions. What is important is to pick up only relevant ones, group them and distil them to ensure their significant applicability.

In the absence of application, ideas remain thoughts, merely stimulating intellectual discussion and gaining appreciation. Normally, around fifty per cent of ideas get accepted while only ten per cent of the accepted ideas are embraced for implementation. The implementation rate is relatively high if the ideas are meant to solve acute problems, rather than the chronic ones, primarily since the former demands immediate firefighting initiatives.

It is observed that organizations are more likely to accept ideas when they originate from external sources. Possibly, the conceptual thoughts of employees are likely to get either blocked or somewhat clouded overtime, and it is often found beneficial to periodically supplement such in-house efforts with inputs from external sources.

Most leading organizations look for consultants to supplement their in-house efforts. Consultants have a broader perception on the subject and can analyse any situation more objectively and without any bias. They have no axe to grind and can therefore critically look into the issues involved. However, satisfaction over consultants' inputs at times is disputable. They often provide solutions that are highly theoretical, with little or limited practical value.

Leading organizations, thus, lean more on facilitators, both in-house and external. Facilitation is both an art and science. It helps managements to demonstrate leadership commitment and strategy, strict compliance to process approaches, their deployment, and interpretation of results related to customers, suppliers and other stakeholders.

Knowledge workers are often invited to provide additional inputs for performance measurement, analysis and enhancement. Such help is always beneficial to all levels of an organization.

It is likely that even the knowledge workers bring in abstractism, without looking into the practical aspects for implementation of their ideas. Such an approach sounds great in theory, but fails during application.

When abstractism rides high, the casualty is credibility. Acceptance of inputs from the knowledge workers, by all levels of the organization, will then be lukewarm. It will then take lot of time to recover lost ground and, over a period, the importance of the inputs will get diluted.

In spite of the above pitfalls, resource persons are often invited by senior managements for providing necessary inputs for a detailed assessment before decision-making. Their analytical abilities are continuously put to the test through several leading questions that could help management in making right decisions. They could either be technical experts or just facilitators with a keen eye for detail.

Such resource persons providing ideas are expected to articulate and convey, in clear terms, what they want to say. Their inputs should be cohesive, logical and workable. They can't afford to be run-of-the-mill types. The inputs are application-oriented, continuously enthuse managements, and encourage them to refine their working with concentration and commitment.

APPLICATION

By mid-1960s, Mukand Steel Foundry, the largest steel casting unit in the country, was positioning itself as a technology leader, with its Research Centre providing the fine edge. Its leadership in the chosen areas of operation was undisputed. It was time for the company to also look into totally new technologies, while holding on to its well-developed strengths. "Heavy Castings" was one such area.

With the installed maximum steel melting furnace capacity of 5 tonnes, the liquid steel that could be handled, at a time, was restricted to that quantity. The entire tonnage of liquid metal, when cast into a sand mould, was taking an hour or so, for complete solidification into solid casting. Whenever castings of bigger sizes were required, customers had no option than to look for sources other than Mukand, including imports.

During that period, the growing market for heavy castings beyond Mukand's capacity, was getting established due to enhanced machine-building activity in the country. The Mukand management considered taking up the production of heavy castings in order to hold on to its leadership position. While the obvious choice was to install suitable larger melting furnaces, Mukand's technology management decided to look into other possible options.

Lateral thinking was the name of the game. Several ideas were generated from the technical team. Every single idea was deliberated with an open mind. Some of them were turned down as not technically feasible while a few others as impractical. Among the short-listed ones, the idea that appealed most was to slow down the solidification process in the mould to such an extent that it would be possible to melt another 5 tonnes of liquid steel and pour into the same mould while the first lot of 5 tonnes was still getting solidified.

Though this idea appeared technically feasible, concerns for its success were too many, including logistics. The problems, likely to be encountered, were mostly anticipatory and not based on previous experience. Further, everyone was certain that the success of the experiment could be established only after a large casting, of well over 5 tonnes, was successfully cast and taken out of the mould. In case of failure, the damage could be enormous. But the management decided to go ahead with implementing the idea.

Bigger sized mould boxes were fabricated in-house. Sand mould mixes were redesigned to meet the increasing metallo-static head requirements. An extensive checklist was prepared and strictly adhered to by all concerned departments. Two liquid-metal-handling overhead travelling cranes, each of 5 tonnes liquid metal capacity, were aligned in series to handle larger casting weights. At every stage of this development, even a minutest detail was carefully examined.

Finally, at the review meeting before the casting D-day, though all possible preparatory steps appeared to have been taken, none of the team members appeared confident of making it a sure success.

At the initiative of late Dr. Joshi, the dynamic team leader, a bright, fresh and young metallurgist was called in to facilitate the team and enthuse them with positive thoughts of confidence. The young boy, though not a foundryman by himself, suggested attaching a vertical parasite to the parent mould cavity.

The metal movement upward in the parasite, visible to naked eye, meant that metal was flowing well in the parent mould also. Once the casting was fully solidified, he said, the parasite could be cut-off, like the appendix in human body.

There was a round of applause on this suggestion, with smiles all-round. The suggestion was successfully implemented. The rest, as they say, is history — of Heavy Steel castings — at Mukand.

KEY LEARNING

Blend your left and right hemispheres. Translate creativity and ideas into workable, practical solutions.

1.4 RESPECT SOCIETY

Every organization needs to be a corporate citizen. Society plays a key role in organizational performance.

APPRECIATION

Organizations cannot operate in isolation. Society has a major role to play in their performance. Hence, organizations cannot ignore societal aspects.

Societal focus has to be a part of organizational philosophy. Once the management includes social responsibility into its daily functioning, it will initiate a structural approach towards planning and implementing to become a corporate citizen. Societal Focus Cells, directly responsible to Chief Operating Officers, ensure necessary organizational thrust.

Such cells proactively move through people, identify their needs and aspirations, work out budgets and implement programmes through systems. All over the world, there are many underprivileged pockets needing help. Physically and mentally challenged persons, children affected by malnutrition, and needy localities can be adopted for such a focussed approach.

Globally, business excellence models are encouraging individuals and organizations towards adaptation of corporate citizenship. All these models encourage leadership to think and appreciate that their individual businesses are not standalones, but are integrated with societal needs. It is the society that provides the necessary environment, which is meaningful to the business. Further, markets are created by the society and leadership must recognize its needs and evolve an appropriate framework to meet those needs.

Enlightened Indian managements are focusing on initiating a large number of activities relevant to both current and futuristic needs of the society. Their commitment towards society is getting demonstrated through a number of initiatives, such as keeping aside a certain percentage of net annual profits as societal budget. There are some organizations who are budgeting a part of total employee cost towards societal expense.

When such a corporate citizenship is demonstrated, organizations can develop annual plans to ensure that the budgeted amounts are appropriately utilized for the needy. Quite often, management of such societal initiatives is given to either the administration or human resource departments. Proper utilization of allocated funds is ensured through periodic reviews with appropriate course corrections.

APPLICATION

Let me recall here the beautiful story published in Sin Min Daily News.

Sixty-seven-year-old Lee Lam of Singapore is a taxi driver, committed to his profession. Honest to the core, he was content and kept his family expenses well within his budget.

Esther Chan, on getting into his taxi, found Lee a decent gentleman and so told him a bit of her story: that she was a heart patient, that she was undergoing treatment and that most taxi drivers refused to take her when they noticed that she looked so sickly.

Lee, who had been plying his cab for more than forty years, was moved. He offered to drive her daily to her office and back. He even said that he would take her to the hospital whenever needed. And all this for free!

For more than a year Lee drove Esther to her workplace at the Registrar of Marriages, eight kilometres away and back. Whenever needed, he took her to hospital and patiently waited to bring her back.

Esther Chan died in November 1993. She was then just forty. But, before she died, Esther gave Lee 2,00 Singapore dollars in gift money and left him a further 500 dollars at her death. In March 1994, Lee received 500 dollars more when he was awarded the Guinness Stout Effort Award for his compassion.

Lee, however, living as he does with his wife and three of his nine children in a two-room apartment, promptly gave the 1,200 dollars plus 500 dollars of his own to charity.

KEY LEARNING

Individuals, organizations and society cannot be mutually exclusive. They are parts of a single entity.

1.5 EMBRACE APPROPRIATE APPROACHES

There are pros and cons for each process improvement method. Implement only those of relevance.

APPRECIATION

Performance management methods have to be carefully selected and implemented to yield significant benefits for an organization. Each method has its own positives and negatives, and its usefulness to an organization depends on its culture and the desired benefits.

To ensure that the deployed methods bring out anticipated benefits, it is essential that they are aligned to organizational needs. When such an alignment is planned and executed, the approaches will be significant and get recognized as an important component of overall management structure.

Once organizations declare core values, they are considered sacrosanct while deciding on management methods for improvement.

Experience has shown that some of the established process enhancement practices like Juran's Trilogy, Crosby's Zero Defects and Deming's 14 Points, need course corrections, modifications and adaptations while implementing in the Indian context. Blindly following any such established performance management method is unlikely to ensure desired benefits.

More importantly, before introducing any new method, it is essential to appreciate the management methods already being followed by the individual functions of an organization. The departmental heads, with their own likes and dislikes, and with their own perceptions provide different directions, in line with their own thoughts and views.

Surely, it is not difficult to adjust and adapt new methods to meet varying demands on the organization. While the available performance enhancement methods are many, and one can choose the best method to meet specific requirements, once the organization selects a particular method in line with the expectations of its stakeholders, it is easy to drive the team towards success, with appropriate course corrections.

The failure in implementation, if any, is primarily due to lack of commitment and absence of data-based management. Unfortunately, many managers continue to function in the firefighting mode and then relish the resultant appreciation and the feeling that it is they who solved the problems. They get activated as and when problems emerge.

When that happens, importance is naturally given to quick-fix solutions. Most process improvement methods can be applied in both reactive and proactive situations, though proactive approaches are far superior to reactive ones.

APPLICATION

The oft-told story of the thirsty crow, with "Self Help" as a core value, is relevant even today.

Once upon a time, a thirsty crow was flying in a jungle looking for water. Even after flying for long, he did not find water. The crow was getting increasingly thirsty. He was desperate, but did not give up. At last, when he saw a big jug under a tree, he was extremely happy.

The crow sat on the rim of the jug and peered inside. Sure enough, there was some water — but not much, just a little quantity at the bottom. The water was at a low level, and in spite of his best efforts, he could not reach it.

For a moment, the crow thought that he would never get to drink water. He needed to do something soon for his own survival. While he pondered over the situation, he looked around. The only thing he could see was a heap of pebbles nearby.

How could the pebbles quench his thirst? Though at first it appeared that water and pebbles were totally unrelated, the crow thought of a fantastic solution. Ah! In the crow's mind, water and pebbles can supplement each other to reach an immediate solution.

The crow picked up one pebble and dropped it into the jug. He then picked up the second pebble from the heap and did the same. Then, the third, the fourth, the fifth and so on. In quick succession, the crow dropped many pebbles into the jug. The pebbles, being heavy, settled at the bottom, and made the water level rise slowly and yet steadily to the top of the jug.

The crow quenched his thirst and flew away happily.

KEY LEARNING

All initiatives need to enhance competence. Absence of commitment and measurements encourage non-cohesiveness among improvement teams.

1.6 TREAT CUSTOMER SOVEREIGN

Customer sovereignty is the key. Evolve dynamic models to manage quality of performance that focuses on customers, and meets their needs and wants.

APPRECIATION

Successful organizations consistently meet customers' needs and expectations, both stated and implied. In the prevailing ruthless competition, it is an essential component for management leadership.

The idea that 'Customer is the King' puts the focus on customer sovereignty. A large number of enlightened corporations have, of late, brought in customer sovereignty as a key corporate value and evolved application models to demonstrate structured progress in that direction.

Once a 'customer-sovereignty'-driven model is evolved, it is easier to develop suitable processes for improving performances, focusing on the customers and their demands.

Customer sovereignty means every employee in the organization believes that increasing customer franchise and loyalty is the only way to meet business objectives, and uses this belief to continually and innovatively exceed customer expectations. The most significant part of this definition is the 'belief' that employees carry about the importance of customer sovereignty. This belief comes only through the processes of leadership, culture building and influencing attitudes.

Implementation of any customer sovereignty model is based on creating a knowledge pack that covers all aspects of relevance, followed by a template which the management can use to execute it. The management can then review the extent the customer sovereignty model has been internalized within the organization.

The quality of implementation will ultimately determine the success of this approach and also have a direct bearing on the credibility of the management in the eyes of employees. Such an approach is not something that an organization should follow independent of its regular work but integrated into it.

There are five distinct areas that would contribute to the successful implementation of customer sovereignty approach. They include leadership culture and attitudes, customer knowledge, value proposition, customer interface and attention to metrics and measurement.

Culture, leadership and attitudes create the basic fabric for the climate within an organization that encourages customer primacy. This fundamental organizational premise is woven into every aspect of its functioning and reflects in not only what the organization does with regard to its customers but also how it does that.

Customer knowledge refers to capturing all the relevant information which helps in understanding what the customer wants, needs and values most, and making it available consistently at all customer touch points. This customer knowledge helps create new approaches, thus exceeding the customer's expectations.

Service offer and value proposition refers to the service promise that the organization makes to its potential customers. It is this premise that an organization communicates to its customers in its advertisements, mailers, and other promotions.

Customer interface refers to every occasion of interaction with the customer. Commercial offers, proposals, quotations, sale, delivery, invoicing, collection, and even customer complaints are all transaction points where an organization interfaces with its customers. These interactions may be face-to-face, over the telephone, over on-line systems, internet, or through simple mail of fax messages.

Metrics and measurements are the most important areas in the successful implementation of customer sovereignty programmes. Anything that can be measured can be monitored, and anything that can be monitored can be managed.

APPLICATION

A senior director of a leading pharmaceutical company and his deputy were one day travelling together in the comfort and luxury of Shatabdi Express departing from Mumbai. Being a part of the same organization ensured enough scope and depth for their conversation.

It is a privilege to travel in such a train, especially in its first-class air-conditioned coupe. There, every passenger is treated like a Maharaja. The ambience provides just the right setting to discuss many subjects, more irrelevant than relevant, throughout the journey.

The beauty of travelling in that comfort is the aroma of sophistication around. It is amusing to listen to the most enlightened passengers sharing their vast knowledge and invaluable experience with co-passengers.

More importantly, every passenger is from a privileged lot and no one questions the other person's wisdom. The passengers believe that his or her inputs are enhancing individual knowledge at a micro-level and serving the nation's cause at a macro-level.

While the senior director and his deputy were in a serious and animated discussion, they found, to their horror, a rat running restlessly in the cabin. Naturally, this intrusion left the two men breathless and the rat became the immediate focus of their discussion.

Memories of a rat-triggered plague that caused havoc a decade ago in Surat, a city close to Ahmedabad, further dampened the spirits of these top executives.

Both shouted for the cabin attendant almost in one voice, ordering the immediate elimination of the rat. They threatened the attendant that his job would be at stake if he did not comply and, more importantly, that he could forget the 100 Rupee tip, a routine whenever they travelled on that train.

The attendant knew they were important and frequent travellers, and promised immediate corrective action.

The gentlemen were delighted when the attendant soon returned and painstakingly spread a newspaper sheet on the carpet, ensuring no folds remained. The curious passengers refrained from distracting the attendant from his attentive work, but once he was done, asked rather sheepishly for the explanation of the experiment.

The attendant said that he had simply spread a newspaper that had quick-fix glue applied all over it. He was certain, that whenever the rat ran over the paper, it would get stuck and its movements restricted. He promised that thus, the menacing rat would soon be caught.

The director and the deputy were thrilled. They continued their conversation, with a rat-free mind.

Four hours later, just before alighting at Ahmedabad, the deputy suddenly remembered the rat when he saw the attendant neatly folding back the newspaper. The deputy enquired inquisitively as to what had happened to the rat, fairly certain that it was caught since it did not disturb them the rest of the journey.

But, the distinguished travellers were dismayed when the attendant revealed he had been using the same paper with the dried-up quick-fix glue for many journeys.

They were disappointed at not being the first to get such a quality service.

KEY LEARNING

The customer is the king. He commands respect, preferred service and deliverables of the highest order.

1.7 REMEMBER ALL STAKEHOLDERS

Everyone who holds a stake in the activities of an individual or an organization can influence their well-being.

APPRECIATION

Are you comfortable in identifying your stakeholders and working towards meeting their expectations? Do you know, at least, your primary stakeholders? Possibly, the answer for such inconvenient questions is a convenient "no." Most of us might not even have addressed these questions since we are not conscious of all our direct contacts and don't think about our distant ones.

Most practicing managers are content with being attentive to the inputs from their suppliers and processing them into such outputs that meet the expectations of their customers. Once this is accomplished, it is normally understood that the job is well done.

Leading performers do not think of their spheres of activity from such a narrow sense. They make conscious efforts to address all stakeholders.

The five primary stakeholders for most organizations are customers, employees, suppliers, lenders and shareholders, though the order of their importance may vary depending on the organizational culture.

These stakeholders have a direct interest in the health of the organizations they are associated with. Their contributions are immense and the benefits are shared. Though specific responsibilities vary and their interests appear distinctive, the outcome is often the result of a coordinated effort.

Over a period, attention to primary stakeholders progressed to higher levels of involvement. Outstanding organizations no longer treat customers as just buyers, but give the utmost respect with customer sovereignty as an organizational core value.

Personnel management has given way to human resource management, with a focus on empowerment and motivation. Suppliers are being recognized as an extended arm of the organizational set up, with conventional inspection giving way to self-certification.

Lending institutions no longer squeeze till the last drop from the companies they lend, but add on to enhance their financial health. Owners are moving out from the profit – only policies to wealth-sharing policies.

Secondary stakeholders are those not having a direct interaction with the organizations, but with the primary stakeholders. Customers' customers, suppliers' suppliers, families of employees, parents for educational institutions, depositor public in financial institutions are among those falling into this category.

Service organizations, including the retail industry need to address the expectations of these secondary stakeholders, since they make a profound impact on the buying habits relevant to these organizations.

Enlightened managements, thus address not only their immediate contacts, but recognize that no single stakeholder is a standalone and his interests are integrated with several others. A careful look at this approach brings out several interested parties needing attention, including society.

APPLICATION

In January 1997, Rani Jethmalani, daughter of former Union Minister, Ram Jethmalani, had almost given up hope of living. She had been in a hospital in London for a year suffering from a collapsed liver.

Search in the UK and USA for an organ transplant seemed futile when suddenly, there came an offer of a matching liver from a young brain-dead accident victim. Jethmalani senior could not make-up his mind on the offer but his son, Rani's brother, took the decision and Rani received the liver transplant.

Today Jethmalani's son is a part of a growing movement to promote Cadaver Organ Transplantation in India. What originally started as an inescapable family need now reached out to all those in such a need.

In fact, the Hope Foundation launched by him, in collaboration with a team of doctors in New Delhi in July 2000 is one of a dozen-odd organizations promoting organ-harvesting from brain-dead victims.

The Hope Foundation follows "the path of successful organ-harvesting centres like Chennai Mohan Foundation and the recently-resurrected Organ Retrieved Banking Organization (ORBO) at the All-India Institute of the exploitative and illicit trade of taking organs from the poor and the destitute, apart from saving lives and inculcating a sense of giving."

The possibilities of organ donation are impressive. At least 47 organs and live tissues can be transplanted from just one cadaver, including the heart, liver, the kidneys, skin, tissue, bone marrow and stem cells, according to a news item published in *The New Indian Express* of 26 June, 2001.

KEY LEARNING

Be aware of your responsibility to stakeholders. Reach out to them.

2 Chapter

BE READY TO CHANGE

Human life, and not just businesses, is constantly affected by change. Anticipating and managing change is an attitude.

CONTENTS

2.1 CHANGE YOU MUST

Constantly change for better. The only thing that does not change in this world is "Change."

APPRECIATION

Change you must, but change before you must!

Managing for performance excellence is never static. Its dynamism is conspicuous to all those closely involved in the change process. In every related area, whether it concerns concepts or practices, there are several continuous improvements made possible only through visible changes.

Change managements continuously look at the company's focus, processes, its products, its attitudes and behaviour, among others. Nothing will remain tomorrow as it is today. This calls for making the organization far more flexible and competitive.

Most organizational activities are primarily customer and market-driven. Customer demands and market expectations are never static – they are constantly changing. Thus, managements-driven by them cannot afford to be static. Senior managements must be the change agents, rather than fear the change. Outstanding CEOs like Jack Welsh looked at change as an opportunity and considered it a necessary constituent in competition.

Change is simply a part of life, and certainly a part of business. How organizations feel about change and how they manage it, greatly impacts the success of the company and pushes it to the forefront. Most people don't like change. When companies appear to be doing fine, they don't appreciate the reason for change.

We are aware that customers and competition are continuously changing. Even the nature of change is changing. Moreover, the pace of change has accelerated. With globalization of economy, companies are facing an increasingly large number of competitors and conflicting customer preferences.

Change is a never-ending journey since the world never stops changing. When changes outside the environment are taking place much faster than a business reacting to it, it is a sure sign of a steep slide.

Change does not always have to upset things and make things worse. In business, change is often the spark that ignites a good idea or a new business opportunity or a revolutionary new product.

It is not only the change that one should address but also the dynamics of change. In a fierce competition, only those who quickly respond to the changing needs will excel. Recognition of this imperative will lead to a proactive approach that constantly ensures change processes.

A study of twenty-six companies over a prolonged period revealed that "organizational adaptation is likely to be characterized by periods of dramatic revolution in which there are changes in a significantly large number of variables, like strategy and structure. Organizations seem to evolve in a manner that is quite similar to the development of scientific knowledge."

APPLICATION

On 20 October, 2006, before The Commonwealth Club of California, Carly Florina, a former Chair and CEO of Hewlett-Packard and the author of *Tough Choices: A Memoir*, talked on "A Prescription for Change".

When Carly came to Silicon Valley in 1999, the mandate was to transform the iconic and legendary company. It was felt that the company needed a massive transformation. The change process Carly led at HP happened at a very particular time in the industry. The industry had a dot-com and then a dot-com bust. It had the worst technology recession in twenty-five years. The market was bearish. The company had announced its merger with Compaq just a week before September 11. It was a tough time to transform a company.

The management, under Carly Florina, decided to go back to its fundamentals, such as innovation, and spread the word that they value these fundamentals. Investments were made and measurements were put in place. The company started generating 3 patents a day in 2001, 5 in 2002, 11 in the years 2003 and 2004, and HP became the number three inventor in the world.

Further, HP progressed from an insular bureaucracy to a performance-focussed meritocracy. The company consolidated its operations so that it could serve customers and introduce a discipline for what the company called a Total Customer Experience.

In advice to other executives, Carly said, "I understand that when you lay off 30,000 people, some of them will not be happy with you. And when you say to people, yes, this is a great company and Bill Hewlett and Dave Packard were great men, but we must move forward – not everyone's going to like you. So you have to step back and say, what am I here for? What is my job? For all those hateful things that were said, I still get, to this day, hundreds and hundreds of messages from people who understand, and who support, and who are happy that we did what we did".

KEY LEARNING

It is not the change, but the dynamics of change that keeps performance management as a challenge.

2.2 KNOW THAT CULTURES DIFFER

Study the culture of your own and sister organizations. All management initiatives have to be in line with the culture.

APPRECIATION

Each organization is unique. The displayed behaviour patterns reflect its culture. India, with its vastness, offers tremendous diversity, and several of its companies have facilities across the country and outside, including in the neighbouring countries. They provide conflicting and dynamically changing regional factors influencing the cultural aspects of these organizations.

Local issues, political pressures, distinctive employee profiles and their backgrounds, lifestyles and community behaviour have a profound influence on the culture of an organization. In most companies, many of these diverse factors are conspicuous, and the extent of their influence often baffles the senior management. Such diversity brings in its own set of problems and constraints which need to be addressed while managing for leadership.

The larger the business group, the greater is the diversity. Big business groups may have, under one umbrella, companies which are over hundred years old to just a year old young ones, and technologically, sunset and sunrise units. The facilities that have been set up may be based totally on indigenous know-how or through strategic alliances with global partners. It is but natural for such diversity to affect the culture of the business group.

It is important to study these characteristics and the cultures of individual organizations and evolve an appropriate group performance strategy, keeping in mind the environment in which the individual organizations are operating. A set of successful models applied in one organization need not necessarily ensure positive results in the other.

Exercises like SWOT analysis, which look into strengths, weaknesses, opportunities and threats, relevant to performance management, highlights the need for each company to initiate and focus on appropriate approaches, with related measurements, covering each activity. Invariably, such approaches are company-centric, evolved after careful consideration of the cultural needs.

Enlightened corporate managements appreciate this imperative. They do not impose a single common approach to their operational units, but rather provide each unit just a set of guidelines with the freedom to adapt to local requirements.

Instead of interfering from the top, they attempt to understand the culture of each unit, facilitate them in implementation of chosen methodologies and integrate them at the corporate level, through factual analysis.

When such an approach is followed, the corporate management will be highly credible both in the supervision of deployment and in the interpretation of the results.

APPLICATION

When we think of cultural differences, the following story should make an interesting reading:

I had just joined the metallurgical engineering department at The Indian Institute of Technology, Bombay, a leading school in India established with Soviet collaboration. For the initial four years, we had professors from the Moscow Institute of Technology, as a collaborative effort, for both teaching and for setting up the laboratory for research work.

Before arriving on deputation, it was mandatory for them to go through a crash course in technical and spoken English. While some were very language-savvy, there were quite a few who were experiencing a great difficulty in overcoming the language barrier.

We had this specialist professor Gudchenko, an expert in heat treatment of metals and alloys. He was a darling professor, highly popular with the students. By the time he landed in India, he had varied experience on both the theoretical and practical aspects of the subject. Students were quite attentive in his class since he always supplemented the theory with several relevant practical examples. He was extremely knowledgeable and pleasantly disposed.

When he entered the campus, like most other professors, his spoken English was somewhat disjointed. He struggled a lot to make himself understood. His pronunciation was difficult to comprehend. But, within four weeks or so, he had substantially overcome this deficiency. He was soon rated as the best professor in spoken English too. Surprisingly, he even learnt the diction of Indian English.

A few weeks later, Gudchenko wanted to have a haircut. He enquired with his friends if there was any barbershop nearby. He was pleased to learn that a new one had just opened opposite the main gate of the institute and the owner could also speak English, apart from Hindi and Marathi, the local languages. Someone even suggested that since he was a foreigner, the barber would possibly give him a special cut at the same cost.

Gudchenko walked into the barbershop. Being from a friendly country, he was received with special attention. The politeness of the shop staff immensely impressed Gudchenko.

Being a new shop, it looked very clean and neat. The furniture and its decor were most pleasing. The three split air-conditioners, installed at right locations, ensured comfortable ambience.

With skilful hands, the barber went about his job with a professional touch. While he worked, the barber had an animated conversation with Gudchenko and shared lot of information about Bombay, later rechristened Mumbai, and its surroundings, the visitor locations and places interesting to foreign tourists.

Once the job was done, the professor asked how much he should pay. The barber pointed to the tariff board that showed rupees ten for a haircut. Gudchenko removed from his pocket a ten-rupee note and a two-rupee one, the later as a tip, and enquired if it was okay.

The barber was all in smiles, vigorously shaking his head in a horizontal direction.

Gudchenko thought the barber was not satisfied with the tip and handed over one more two-rupee note. The barber was sure grinning and still kept on moving his head horizontally and with greater frequency. The good professor was at a loss. He didn't know how to get out of this predicament.

He decided the best thing to do was give him another two-rupee note and quickly run out of the shop. Which he did!

When he narrated the incident to his students, everyone had a hearty laugh. While in Soviet Union, one expresses appreciation by shaking the head vertical, it is the reverse in India.

Gudchenko had now learnt an important cultural difference.

KEY LEARNING

Organizational culture is conspicuous everywhere; in barber shops to table tops and even in toilet blocks.

2.3 BE CREDIBLE

Demonstrated credibility across the organization, at both vertical and horizontal levels, is vital for the success of performance management.

APPRECIATION

Performance can be enhanced when the management demonstrates an increasing credibility through the right communication, positive attitude and behaviour. While it is relatively easy at an individual level, organizational credibility needs to be cultivated and demonstrated across all functions and by all employees. It can neither be an isolated practice nor a secretive execution.

The management must continue to direct its efforts positively in establishing credibility towards the needs and aspirations of internal and external customers at all levels.

Demonstrated honest communication is straightforward and comprehensive and is not restricted to certain organizational or functional levels. It extends to the organization as a whole. To ensure visible credibility, the management demonstrates its commitment by avoiding pitfalls, often demonstrated only through honest assessments, and riding on the positives while overcoming the weaknesses.

A projection of honesty, integrity and positive belief to all stakeholders is easier said than done. Organizations should encourage employees to communicate honestly about what they wish to say rather than trying to paint a tutored and favourable — but untrue — picture of themselves and the organization.

When anything is portrayed inaccurately, it will reflect negatively on organizational credibility. Why force anyone into a position that could later prove embarrassing for him and his employer?

This point of honest communication has been brought up by Norman King in his book, while summarizing a rather interesting study on human psychology. Norman King highlights basically two types of people: those who want to fit in at all costs, and those who care little about fitting in. Tests showed that both characteristics are present in all of us, but when one of them dominates the other, it reflects in our prominent behaviour.

In businesses, one must be able to talk honestly. But, it is not easy to hide feelings behind a mask of politeness and conceal private thoughts from others. Business intimacy means that you must subject yourself to a certain risk of vulnerability.

However, while honesty and accuracy are important in establishing oneself in any relationships, there is a certain level of self-disclosure that should not be conveyed in the initial moments of a business relationship. One needs to make disclosures extremely carefully, without being too self-revealing and detailed.

Often, we come across, within large corporates, some group management functions whose credibility with the group companies need much to be desired. Experience shows that these functions should not boss over or police the individual companies or be faultfinding.

Instead, they should be supportive at all levels. When deficiencies are observed, the corporate management should approach these companies as internal customers for solutions and suggest areas for improvement.

One attribute that needs to be completely curbed is the 'I-know-all' approach. Human behaviour gets appreciated when intraorganizational communications are honest, fact-based and value-added.

Accuracy of information and correctness of feedback are two vital components in ensuring credibility in every management function. Such a feedback should be defect- free and should withstand organizational scrutiny, audits and assessments.

APPLICATION

It was the period when I was heading a strategic business unit in a steel foundry in India, specialising in the production of castings required for the Indian Railways. As a part of the export responsibility, I had a great experience with the Industry Ministry of the then Soviet Union where everyone dealt with me, an Indian, in a very friendly manner. Government and non-government sources went out of their way to make my frequent visits to Moscow enjoyable, comfortable and beneficial.

During my initial visits, I developed excellent professional and personal contacts with senior officials of the industry and steel ministries, especially with the Industry Minister Abramowsky. Soon, I could seek and get appointments from the minister's office without even going through normal protocol. The rapport worked wonders.

Once the Soviet Union's intent to import alloy steel castings for its large railway network was crystallized, we started making our commercial moves. We ensured that our technical offer was in line with their stringent requirements. Several rounds of technical meetings were followed by negotiations with commercial officials. In the end, the company's name was shortlisted for the final round scheduled in the presence of the honourable minister.

On D-day, we were invited to meet Abramowsky and his team of officials. For that clinching event, I requested Shah, the company's Chief Executive to come over to Moscow and finalise the deal. He arrived from Bombay by the evening flight and we had our preparatory meeting over dinner. The next morning at 10 o'clock, we were preparing to go to Kremlin. Shah came out of his hotel room smartly dressed in a suit and tie, while I was in an informal attire. He appeared somewhat annoyed and asked why I was not also formally dressed.

At that time, I was not comfortable with the idea of dressing up formally. Moscow was extremely hot during that season. I knew that the visitors' room, where one would wait before being ushered into the minister's comfortable chambers was hot, humid and sometimes stuffy.

Shah asserted it was vital for the company to get that export order and we should not take any chances with this most important prospective customer. He still believed that formal attire was the need of the occasion.

While politely telling him that I had already developed a personal rapport with all key members of the negotiating team and reminding him of the scorching heat, my bottom line statement was if wearing a tie and suit could fetch me a contract, I would not mind wearing even five jackets at a time.

Shah smiled at this logic and did not press further. We left for the appointment. The honourable minister received us with open arms, mentioned repeatedly that he and his colleagues were extremely impressed with our organization, its technical capability and negotiating skills. More importantly, the minister said, that our company displayed the highest credibility with the Soviet team.

Shah was all smiles when we walked out with the contract.

KEY LEARNING

Be friendly,communicative and reliable. There is nothing to be secretive about while sharing organizational competence.

2.4 MAKE A MARK

Focus on personal quality. It cannot be separated from organizational quality. Individual output is an integral part of organizational output.

APPRECIATION

Employees are an integral part of an organization. Their attitude, beliefs, behaviour and performance have a direct bearing on the organizational health. Organizational quality and employee quality are two sides of the same coin. They are inseparable.

Attention to personal quality ensures sustained results. Adaptation of organizational development models that integrate on-the-job and attitude-related training for employees, at all levels, contribute to personal quality. Only the focus on enhancement of quality-related attributes can ensure improvement in quality of personnel, to the delight of all stakeholders.

Quality of an individual can easily be recognized and emulated by his associates. Issues such as time, discipline, respecting one another, activity focus, commitment to self and the organization, respecting society and national pride are some of the softer skills that should be addressed to enhance personal quality.

Just as organizational quality is managed for its benefits, both tangibles and intangibles, financial and non-financial, the effectiveness of personal quality models can also be measured based on the value addition in dealing with others in the organization.

The employees should perceive that it is beneficial for them to be proactive and continuously derive enjoyment while improving their performance levels.

Many organizations look at manpower as a burden. Such an approach results in imbalance in the employer-employee relationships. Enlightened organizations have adopted a system of open communication and have started sharing even the financial health of the organization. Such open communication helps in integrating personal quality with organizational quality.

Individuals who make a mark in any organizational hierarchy have distinct styles of their own. However, all of them are charming, confident, forceful, casual and yet authoritative. While they are good listeners and communicative, they are also assertive.

In the final analysis, they come out in flying colours due to their most impressive results. They proactively maximize their impact and inspire confidence and commitment among others.

APPLICATION

Reddy and Sharma were senior executives in a leading Indian bank. They were neighbours staying in the same housing complex of sixty bungalows, a luxury according to Mumbai's living standards. Reddy was in the marketing field, high-flying, dominating, talkative and communicative, while Sharma was a computing specialist, a quiet person providing back-up support to banking operations.

One morning, during the rush hour, the two were travelling to office in Sharma's car. When they reached a busy corner, Reddy suddenly remembered that he had earlier promised a friend, staying a few blocks ahead, a lift in his car.

But, Reddy realised that there was no way Sharma could stop, since it was a no-parking zone.

Reddy was restless. He was determined to give his friend the promised lift. Suddenly, he asked Sharma to stop the car in the middle of the road. Sharma was taken aback, and speechlessly did as he was told. Reddy immediately pulled, from inside, the lever to open the bonnet, got down from the vehicle, opened the bonnet fully and pretended as if something was wrong with the engine.

A worried traffic police came towards the vehicle, keen on towing the car to the side of the road to avoid slowing down the traffic. Reddy argued with the cop that with a few attempts the engine might restart, showing he was pretty sure he could fix it soon. As soon as Reddy's friend came running to the car, the engine 'mysteriously' restarted.

Sharma was extremely upset at this unethical and shameful incident. He was uncomfortable throughout the day in the office, though he did not say a word to Reddy, whose chamber was a few yards away on the same floor.

At the end of the day, when Sharma mustered some courage to express his annoyance, Reddy did not show even a hint of regret. His dismissal of the entire episode as a minor incident spoke volumes.

KEY LEARNING

Individuals are ambassadors of organizations. Organizational behaviour is reflected through the attitude of employees.

2.5 BE ON LEARNING MODE

Performances need to be reviewed periodically and constantly improved, with defined responsibilities and targeted completion dates.

APPRECIATION

Leaders constantly strive to identify ways to do work cheaper, faster, smarter and always better than their competitors. Those who don't learn newer and improved ways, find it difficult to stay competitive.

Periodic reviews can make managers keep up with the change, proactively manage process improvements and constantly learn through these experiences.

Leaders need to be highly knowledgeable in understanding business processes and knowing how to change them towards improvement. Effective managers manage processes as well as they lead people. They are the champions of process change and continuous learning.

Objective reviews provide the best learning opportunities, more so when processes are focused, process-flows analyzed and those steps adding value get recognized so that non-value added processes are rid of.

Reviews are the responsibility of those accountable for both processes and their outcome. They would have not only learnt their basic businesses but have a thorough knowledge on how the management processes, relevant to their areas, operate. They need to have a clear understanding of the work processes under their control.

This not only sets the expectation that continuous improvement is an important responsibility, but also provides the basic skills required for such an improvement.

What do leaders do further in reviews? Leaders look at how they did against expectations. They study for variations in customer needs so as to identify which customer need requires a new process. It is far better to create new processes to respond to new customer needs than to have each request with a built-in variation.

Metrics provide appropriate indicators of process health. They talk about internal and external factors that cause the numerical data to fluctuate both positively and negatively. They reject variations that are not cost effective in both quantifiable and non-quantifiable terms.

Metrics explore trends in variations caused by other work groups who may also need to improve their processes.Objective structured reviews are a vital component for continuously improved performances. Structured reviews are indeed a part of management of such performances. Also, a key element of the reviews is to critically look at the progress of implementation on the decisions taken during previous review meetings.

Such reviews also look into modified processes and their effectiveness to the current needs, and evolve appropriate action plans with a targeted responsibility matrix.

Once such a review is institutionalized, persons responsible for a specified activity take total ownership of the implementation. Personal commitment can surely make it happen.

Positive results are achieved when team-members are empowered to complete their tasks.

At the same time, they are encouraged to enhance their own soft skills, such as team working, communication ability and analytical capability.

Many developments are taking place around us and we can't ignore their dynamics. One should constantly observe, listen, understand and implement relevant developments that enable one to be always in the learning mode.

Let us appreciate that in the absence of any significant effort, on an average, we forget 80 per cent of what we learn on any given day.

APPLICATION

On 12 April, 1945, Harry S. Truman received urgent summons from the White House, immediately after president F D Roosevelt had suddenly died. Truman had been vice-president for only eighty-two days and was ill-prepared to take over presidency. Yet, Truman guided United States through one of the most chaotic and testing periods with an insight, optimism and grit that turned him into one of the most effective leaders the country had ever seen.

In 1917, when the United States had entered the World War I, Truman was a farmer near Grandview, Missouri. He was overage and short-sighted, unable to see without glasses. He was not expected to be in the forces, but was drafted when he was thirty-three.

During his presidency, Truman bravely faced head-on a number of challenges that fell upon him, beginning with the fateful decision of dropping an atomic bomb on Hiroshima. The next four-year period of his presidency was dominated by the Korean war and an anti-communist hysteria at home, threatening the very existence of American democracy. Yet, Truman remained steadfast in the principles he cherished.

When Truman entered the Senate in 1935, his plainspoken friendliness, highest integrity, and commitment to his office quickly won respect, trust and affection from both his colleagues and public. While he had a modest record of achievements during his first term, it was during his second Senate term that he gained national spotlight by creating and chairing a committee investigating fraud in the U.S. military and its suppliers. The Truman Committee was ruthless in pulling up military officers, civil administrators and defence contractors to the highest standards of integrity, efficiency and performance.

Truman's Senate record made him an attractive candidate for Roosevelt's running mate in his fourth term campaign of 1944. In July 1945, Harry Truman enjoyed a public approval of 87 per cent. Though when he left his office in January 1953 his approval rating stood at a mere 31 per cent, primarily due to hostile Republican press, he made his mark in world history.

Truman became a great leader in his own right. Several decisions he had to make were momentous, world changing, world building, and, potentially, world destroying.

Truman often said that he was not a born leader, but an "ordinary man". He told an audience of farmers, "I am sure that at the bottom of your heart you know that the ordinary man is the backbone of the country".

His countrymen admire him as a honest leader, good negotiator and a great decision-maker. His experiences can be distilled into principles that modern-day managers can use in their own quest for success.

KEY LEARNING

Continuously learn not only to compete and survive, but to maintain top leadership position

2.6 INNOVATE

Incremental performance enhancement methods may not be sufficient. Innovations during the journey help to outperform.

APPRECIATION

What is best today may not be even good enough tomorrow. By implementing new ideas in all key operations while solving or anticipating the problems, one can achieve remarkable results, thereby enhancing customer satisfaction, increasing profitability, and value for effort for everyone around. Further breakthrough improvements and practices significantly enhance quality of life.

Before diving into any creative challenge-solving process, it is necessary to first evaluate whether the situation at hand would be best solved through a creative thinking process or through more traditional means. A creative solution is helpful when we are not sure how to evaluate a problem, causes are unknown and unpredictable and risky solutions are acceptable.

Creative people engage in undisciplined, open-minded, and uncritical thinking in the initial stages of the problem-solving process. Remaining open-minded allows one to generate more alternates.

Innovation does not necessarily require doing, making or thinking something that did not exist before. Innovative ideas can be generated through out-of-the-box thinking. The tools often applied include brainstorming. Successful leaders encourage innovation by creating a climate in which individuals freely present their ideas without fear of criticism. Fear of criticism is the biggest obstacle to people voicing new ideas.

Both logical and intuitive thinking are necessary for creating the optimum climate for innovation. Logical thinking is a sequential process, while intuitive thinking tends to be holistic. Idea-simulation techniques can also be classified in these ways. To maximize innovative solutions, make sure that the team-members utilise both ways of thinking for generating new ideas.

Innovative and creative ideas are needed not only to solve business problems, but are also necessary ingredients in identifying and creating enhanced products and services and also in creating new and innovative ones.

Albert Einstein once said that common sense is the collection of prejudices acquired by the age eighteen. While talking of breaking the rules, he said, "I sometimes ask myself how it came about that I was the one to develop the theory of relativity. The reason I think is that a normal adult never stops to think about problems of space and time. These are the things which he has thought of as a child. But my intellectual development was retarded, as a result of which I began to wonder about space and time only when I had already grown up".

But, it was not Einstein, the wise old professor, who first solved the mysteries of space and time. He was a kid, just out of college. He worked at the Swiss patent office reviewing improvements to laundry wringers. He did physics on the quiet. Hence, by then he was breaking the rules.

Einstein is reported to have once said that the significant problems we face cannot be solved using the same level of thinking we used when we created them.

Often impossible problems get addressed over and over again, using strategies similar to previous problems, without any success. But one can win over those hopeless problems when one breaks the rules.

APPLICATION

A hare and a tortoise, living in Ahmedabad, were good friends and, like all good friends they sometimes had a dig at each other. One day, in a lighter mood, the hare ridiculed the tortoise for its slow pace. The tortoise reacted by challenging the hare to a race from Paldi to Navarangpura.

On the appointed day and time, the two assembled at the starting line and began the race. The hare dashed off the start line in a flash. After the midway mark, he felt that a short nap would do no harm. The short nap turned out to be a bit too long. Meanwhile the tortoise crossed the hare and reached the destination. The hare woke up from his slumber, oblivious of the time, and dashed to the finish line. To his dismay, he saw the tortoise having a nap at the finish line.

The moral of the story is: "Slow and steady wins the race".

The story does not end here...

The hare went home and soon understood that complacency and overconfidence were the reasons of his defeat. He vowed not to repeat the mistake. He invited the tortoise to another race. The tortoise agreed.

They met at the appointed day and time at the starting line. The race began. This time the hare dashed off to the finish line without a break and won the race comfortably.

The moral of the story is: "Fast and steady wins the race".

The story still does not end here...

The tortoise went home and thought hard. He was aware that the hare could not be defeated in speed. He pondered over his core competence. He found a solution and invited the hare to another race. This time the course was changed. It was from Paldi to the Airport. The hare agreed.

At the appointed day and time, the two met at the start line and the race began. The hare dashed off like a flash and soon arrived at the bank of the river Sabarmati. He was overwhelmed by a sense of dejection, because he did not know how to swim.

The tortoise came to the bank, looked at the hare with sympathy and coolly got into the water. He swam to the other side and went to the airport and returned.

The moral of the story is: "Core competence wins the race".

But the story does not end here either...

The two friends decided that it was enough of racing against each other. They pondered: Why not travel together from Paldi to the Airport in the least amount of time?

At the end of a brainstorming session, they came up with a solution and decided to try it out the next morning. At the appointed time, the two met at the starting line.

The tortoise sat on the back of the hare. The hare dashed off from Paldi to the bank of Sabarmati. There he got onto the back of the tortoise and the tortoise swiftly crossed the river. On reaching the other side, the tortoise sat on the back of the hare again. The hare ran as fast as he could to the airport. Thus, they both reached the airport in the minimum time.

Finally, the moral of the story is: "Innovation and teamwork wins the race".

KEY LEARNING

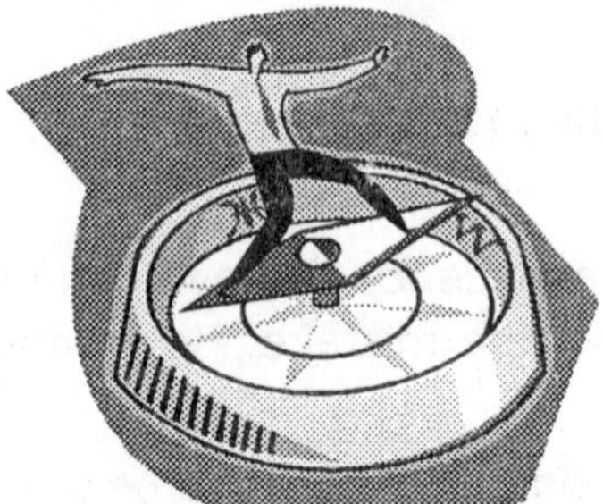

Continuously innovate all processes, all systems and all deliverables.

3

Chapter

IMPROVE THE PROCESSES

Every activity in the universe is a process, with several factors impacting different process steps.

CONTENTS:

3.1 DO PRIORITISE

Focus on a vital few.Do not waste time on the trivial many.

APPRECIATION

It is common knowledge that one who makes a noise gets the maximum attention. Not because he makes sense, but because he creates attracting decibels. Often in a meeting, a few members tend to make the most comments, while others are relatively quiet.

There is a tendency, then, for several trivial aspects to creep in, especially when the inputs are impulse-driven and intuition-based, with little attention to detail. The vital issues are then overlooked.

Experienced managers and professionals usually clearly distinguish vital points from the trivial ones in everyday business situations to enable them to focus essentially on the former. The Pareto diagram is a tool to arrange the available details — not perceptions — according to their importance, and separate the vital few from the trivial many, while addressing any business situation.

The Pareto principle, once applied, appears so obvious and so simple that one wonders why it doesn't get the deserved attention in the first place. After all, everyone knows that when the vital few are focused on, one can aim for the greatest gain in business.

But, if everyone knows it already, why do managers so often complain that they are simultaneously faced with dozens of problems in their organization? Also why do company improvement teams list dozens of problems and set out to solve all of them with equal vigour, at the same time?

Obviously, the culprit is the lack of attention for implementation.

If one really understands and appreciates this simple but profound Pareto principle, the first management step when faced with a host of problems would be to gather data to identify the vital few and then focus improvement efforts on those few things that would give the best benefits.

The Italian Economist, Wilfredo Pareto (1848-1923), during his study on distribution of wealth, observed that 80-90 per cent of Italy's wealth was in the hands of 10-20 per cent of the population. M. G. Lorenz, an US economist further developed a form of cumulative curve to depict the accumulation of such wealth.

It was Dr. Joseph Juran, in the mid-1920s, who observed that quality defects were unequal in frequency and only a few defects accounted for the bulk of the rejections. "Typically, only 20 per cent of the causes are responsible for 80 per cent of the outcome", he observed.

Juran applied the name "Pareto Principle" to this phenomenon of a vital few and what he termed the "useful many", superimposed the Lorenz curve, and demonstrated its universal applicability. This principle is accepted in all areas of organizational performance, including quality, cost, delivery and safety.

Leading performers are convinced that an effective problem recognition measure is not when problems such as high internal rejections, customer returns, customer complaints, lower margins are noticed, but when the senior management believes there is a significant gap between their performance and that of their competitors.

The performance gap can show up at many places, and it is impossible to address all of them at the same time, unless they get prioritized.

APPLICATION

During the early-1950s, India started experiencing a mini-steel plant boom. There was a good demand for steel rods and bars from the nascent Indian construction and engineering industry. The country was under the notorious control and license raj, with restricted manufacturing capacities. Any tonnage produced over and above the licensed capacity needed justification, a sure disincentive to improved productivities. Consequently, well-established bar and rod mills did great business.

Mukand Steel, a leading steel mill located in Bombay, was in the production of bars and rods through straight beds. Its products were well accepted by the user industries, located mostly in and around Bombay. To meet the increasing demand of the Indian construction and engineering industry, more and more mills of similar design were getting installed threatening the competence of Mukand's business.

Mukand skirted around for emerging technologies to stay competitive. The Looping Technology appeared to be promising, aiming at significantly reducing the mill lengths and saving in power by at least by one-fourth. The production costs were also getting reduced by twenty per cent, a significant part of it being due to higher productivities.

Viren Shah, Mukand's CEO, desired to introduce the latest Looping Technology to maintain leadership. In those days such a technology was not available in India and had to be imported.

Appropriate specifications for the plant and machinery were drawn up and global quotations obtained. After detailed deliberation and careful consideration, a blueprint was prepared for implementation. The necessary capital investment was made and the plant was installed with great fanfare.

Since Mukand was already in the steel rolling business, the management thought it would be a cakewalk introducing the Looping Technology. After a few initial hiccups, operations of all key equipment were well standardized. However, the manually operated loopers were ineffective and could not make a smooth looping operation, resulting in in-process material wastage of over thirty per cent, making the plant most uneconomical.

The plant management tried its best to set things right. The operating colleagues considered several variables and looked into all possible reasons for the failure in getting the bars looped. On paper, the looping technology appeared simple. Instead of the straight length rolling that brings down the bar size from around 60 millimetres to 10 millimetres, through multiple reductions in rotating rolls, the rods are required to be looped back by 180 degrees at fixed intervals.

But the problem was the rods were slipping during this looping back operation, resulting in wastage.

After extensive consultations with the management board members, Shah, appointed Mr. Desmet to manage the just-commissioned bar mill. Desmet had considerable hands-on experience on such mills in Europe. He initiated a quick study, looking into all possible variables and their data. On the face of it, everything seemed to be normal to him. Later, he decided on a detailed and in-depth analysis.

He listed every single possible cause, covering all technical and operational issues of relevance to Mukand conditions. He was convinced that enough operational details were already available, and there was no immediate need for fresh experimentation.

He sat down to carefully study the existing data and information. He then eliminated trivial issues after looking into the data and analyzing it through what was then known as the simple ABC analysis. Desmet and his team worked practically the whole day dipping into the available data.

What he concluded was an eye-opener. The maximum problem area was at the looping step itself and the installed looping equipment was incapable of tackling this problem. Even a slight obstacle in the looping path was sufficient to alter the trajectory, causing cut-offs in the rolling process, resulting in huge scrap.

Desmat decided that the mechanical loopers should be replaced by skilled ones. The manual loopers needed to be highly skilled to hold the incoming hot bars in tongs, turn them around 180 degrees and push them into the next groove in the roll. A training facility was developed, simulating this split-second looping operation. Young, bright and physically strong persons were recruited as trainees.

Since he was a hands-on expert, Desmet had the show–how capability and repeatedly demonstrated the simulated training without a single failure. But, none of the trainees could emerge successful from this training. After a week or so, while Mukand's management was getting anxious, Desmet was firm that he could not run the mill if he was not confident of manual looping competence.

The skills required for the manual looping were then prioritized. It was decided that the most important quality one should look for was quickest reflection, and possibly such a quality could be demonstrated only by the best automobile drivers.

The immediate next step was to recruit such people and offer attractive salaries. Training began, and the new recruits were very quick to develop the necessary skills. Thus, the manual looping of steel bars and rods arrived at Mukand.

KEY LEARNING

A good manager prioritizes his activities every minute.

3.2 IMPROVE CONTINUALLY

Remember continual improvements are imperative for exceeding performances. For such improvements, there are no finishing lines.

APPRECIATION

Leading quality organizations are moving well beyond the well known corrective and preventive modes and are looking beyond the established continuous improvement processes. They are now addressing both incremental and breakthrough improvements, as a part of their continual improvement process.

There are two ways of conducting continual process improvements:

- Breakthrough projects which either lead to revision and significant improvement in existing processes or implementation of new processes. Cross-functional teams, outside routine operations, usually carry out these projects.
- Small-step ongoing improvement activities conducted within existing processes.

Continual improvements by either method involve a number of steps. Prominent among them are:

- ⇨ Drive for improvement: both incremental and breakthrough
- ⇨ Analyze current situation
- ⇨ Identify improvement areas
- ⇨ Arrive at possible solutions
- ⇨ Critically evaluate them
- ⇨ Implement and standardize new solutions
- ⇨ Evaluate their effectiveness
- ⇨ Initiate further improvement

Continual improvement process is a powerful and dynamic tool. A strategic objective of an organization can be continual improvements in all its key processes to enhance measurable performances, for the benefit of all stakeholders.

The concept and application of continual improvement, through breakthrough projects, aim to achieve significant beneficial changes within the organization proactively. It is usually done without waiting for problems to throw up opportunities for improvement.

Further, continual improvement attempts to achieve enhanced organizational process-centric results, every time.

APPLICATION

When the top Indian management team returned from Tokyo after attending a one-week training programme conducted by the Union of Japanese Scientists and Engineers, popularly known as JUSE, in the year 1991, the single take-home mantra was "go ahead and continuously improve". The importance of continuous improvement was drilled into the team-members with several stories on how the Japanese had mastered it over the years and how it had become a part of the Japanese culture.

The way Japan went about managing quality as a business strategy, built around proactive continuous improvements, is by now legendary. A large number of books have been published, and continue to be written, on how they had captured the global automobile, steel and electronic businesses, to name only a few.

Japan's transformation, in the 1970s, as a global competitor continued over the last three decades primarily since the country not only mastered the principle of continuous incremental improvements but also introduced several breakthroughs aimed at retaining this leadership in time.

The news item published in San Jose Mercury News of 15 November, 2006 makes for interesting reading. It indeed hides more than what it reveals. The American automobile giants, namely Ford, General Motors and Daimer Christler of Chrysler's group have been, of late, going through a tough time and severe financial crisis. Ford alone reported a third quarter loss of $ 7 billion.

CEOs of the troubled Big Three automakers had met with President Bush the previous day and as they emerged from the meeting saying they had received an understanding hearing, Bush made no commitments, particularly in response to the executives' complaint that Asian countries, notably Japan, were holding their currencies artificially low so that their cars could be cheaper.

In fact, as per the news item, the auto leaders had sought the White House meeting way back in April to air their problems, but the president had not found the time due to the mid-term poll of November.

In addition to trade and currency issues, the automakers and the president discussed fuel efficiency, energy security and alternate fuels. On alternate fuel, as per the report, the executives told Bush that half their fleets could run on ethanol or bio diesel fuel, instead of gasoline, by 2012.

Incidentally, the paper carried on the same day a news item, with a photograph of a stylish fuel-cell Honda Car, also called Hydrogen Car, with Honda declaring that it would put a fuel-cell vehicle into limited production by 2008.

KEY LEARNING

Incremental improvements need to be supported with breakneck breakthroughs to remain competitive on a continuous basis, with speed.

3.3 MAKE PROCESSES LEAN

Bulky processes have an inscrutable appetite to absorb the insignificants, with little to cheer about quality, time and cost dimensions.

APPRECIATION

There are several key management components an organization addresses. These can be broadly grouped under strategies, processes and results.

It is the leadership that provides the strategic intent and expresses its commitment through demonstrated actions. It creates long-term and short-term strategies in line with this commitment and evolves systems that are beneficial to the organization.

Leadership commitment provides the necessary drive for an organization to evolve and implement appropriate operating processes and manage them with horizontal and vertical deployment. It is essential to remember that processes move horizontally from input to output unlike individual departmental activities, which move vertical in a hierarchical manner.

It is the interface between different functions in an organization that provides weak links which are damaging. They often create several roadblocks to outstanding performance. These weak links are addressed by evolving appropriate systems that focus on interface transactions.

Results, both financial and non-financial, are an outcome of leadership drive across the organization and strict compliance to the evolved processes and systems. When the system compliance is conspicuous, the results are consistently positive. In a competing environment, the results are not looked at by leading performers as stand-alone, but are always compared with targets, trends, competitors' data and benchmarks.

Processes like Lean Six Sigma help in not only improving all the processes towards better working, while using the above stated incremental and breakthrough improvement methods, but also look at how work flows from one person or workstation to the next. This eliminates wasteful processes and results in speedy process steps.

Attention to the Lean process provides the necessary drive towards rapid and sustainable gains when systematically worked on high priority projects, linked to the organizational business goals. Applying the principle demands focussed training to all employees with attention to applicable inputs. However, such training alone does not guarantee superior job performance.

Application of what is learnt depends a lot on senior management. While superior executives always train and develop subordinates on their jobs, leading from behind requires a strong commitment to the belief that all individuals are capable to perform with speed, and that the management has a role in providing the right environment and support to make it possible.

APPLICATION

During the 1970s, the Indian steel industry had the dubious distinction of producing steel products at the highest cost. The public sector steel plants had virtual monopoly and all steel users across the country were at their mercy for their requirements, though Tata Steel was the saving grace to a number of downstream units.

A mini steel industry was just taking shape with secondary steel producers, operating through relatively more expensive scrap melting route instead of the primary route with iron-ore as the raw material.

The steel controller maintained the production and despatch figures of all the plants, and penalised any plant producing beyond the licensed capacity. The controller prevented the plants from enhancing productivity and production levels beyond the permitted output.

During that period, the Japanese steel industry was booming. Japan had no iron-ore or any other major raw material required for steel making. Every single item had to be imported. India, with its rich iron-ore deposits, was a major exporter to Japanese steel plants.

Eventually, Japan was importing the most iron-ore from India at Indian price, and exporting steel products to India at a price lower than Indian manufacturing costs. Everyone wondered how the Japanese did it.

The steel ministry of Government of India formed a technical committee to study and report this issue within three months. The first stop was Daido Steel, one of the highly efficient and respected Japanese steel plants. While agreeing to the investigating team's visit, the plant wanted it to enter into a confidentiality agreement, that too on their terms.

I was a member of this team. The Daido management nominated Takahashi to interact with the team. Takahashi had all the data on his finger tips, but he was too secretive and did not release information easily. Initially, we felt that language was the barrier but we soon realised that the Japanese steel industry was really not ready to divulge anything concerning their operations.

Dealing with these plants was a challenge. Direct questions did not get any worthwhile responses. To our frustration, the team was denied direct meetings with several key officials of most plants.

In the end, the team could collect only one tenth of the expected data. In a way, the visit seemed disappointing. But, once we started analysing the available data, there were smiles allround. The team realised the tremendous usefulness of the collected data and information.

The conclusions drawn were quite revealing. The productivity levels of Japanese plants were five times more than the Indian plants, and employee cost per tonne of steel was around three times higher. The strictest control on inventory and on-time planning for optimum product mix were among the key factors that brought down the costs further.

The amused team then found that all the key process steps managed were so lean, the time taken to convert the raw material into the final product and reach customer destination was typically 18 days, in comparison to 45 days in Indian steel plants. The positive financial impact was quite striking, particularly on the so-called working capital, at a time when the ruling Indian institutional lending rate was 18 per cent in comparison to 4 per cent in Japan.

What a great impact in making all operations so lean!

KEY LEARNING

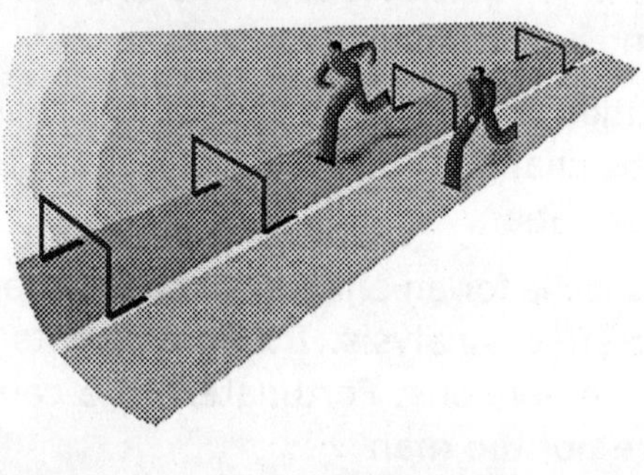

Every activity, from input to output, has several process steps. They need to be leaner, appropriately aligned and measured. That will ensure achieving benchmarked results, as planned.

3.4 DIG INTO THE ROOT-CAUSE

Avoid solving problems through symptoms. Like in medical diagnostics, the importance of the root cause cannot be underestimated.

APPRECIATION

Achieving a desired performance level is the outcome of several factors. For any such effect, there could be several causes, each one affecting the process. Addressing any process improvement, without due consideration of all such causes, will certainly be futile.

Processes cannot be controlled just by shouting, "control, control and control". What it needs is focusing on the process which is a collection of cause factors, as stated by Ishikawa, and within that process find ways of making better products, establishing better goals and achieve enhanced objectives. Improvement teams, when they do not resort to causative analysis, tend to look for quick-fix solutions even while appearing to be applying systematic problem-solving methodologies.

A problem, in its simplest definition, is a condition or a set of circumstances that a person or group or an organization thinks should be changed. Often, problems are the product of human ignorance, dissatisfaction and aspiration.

Usually, the number of causative factors responsible for an effect could be so many that one tends to resort to only a cursory cause-effect analysis. If one attempts to address all the cause factors, the task would be tremendous. Fortunately, the cause factors which would sharply influence an effect are not too many.

But who would decide these most influencing causes? Surely, those most familiar with the process who also should be involved through the most powerful tool of brainstorming. The opinions expressed at such sessions are checked rationally and scientifically against the data available, and analyzed.

When the team's actions are based on symptomatic analysis, the solutions are temporary and problems often recur. Only the root-cause analysis will give permanent and irreversible solutions.

The root-cause analysis needs an in-depth study of all possible causes and an appreciation of the cause-effect chain. Intense training adds understanding and a proper application of necessary tools to achieve a defect-free performance.

The symptomatic problem solving approach does not need any major training and is experience-dependant. In medical terms, it is like allopathic treatment, while the root-cause approach is homoeopathic.

APPLICATION

Once upon a time, there lived a man named Abdul. He would set out in the morning with a head-load of caps and go from village to village selling them.

One hot and humid afternoon, Abdul desired to rest. He set down his bag of caps under a tree, lay down and had a refreshing nap.

When he woke up, all the caps were gone. Abdul was shocked. No one was around, but he heard some screeching noises from the treetop. Abdul looked up. There were many monkeys sitting on the branches of the tree, each wearing a cap.

"How can I get my caps back?" he wondered.

Abdul got an idea. After all, monkeys are monkeys. Attracting the monkeys' attention, he took off his cap. All the monkeys followed his action, and took off their own caps. Then Abdul waved the cap around. The monkeys waved, too. Then, Abdul threw his cap to the ground. All the monkeys threw their caps down. Abdul quickly collected the caps and happily walked away.

The moral of the story is that, there will be hurdles. Find the solution.

But the story didn't end here.

Years passed. Abdul was now an old man and his grandson carried on the cap business.

One day, Abdul said to his grand son, "Listen dear, I wish to caution you". Then he related his monkey trick to his grandson.

The very next day, the grandson was walking from one village to another. He too laid down for a short nap under a tree. When he woke up, he found the monkeys on the treetop, wearing the caps. He remembered his grandpa's advice.

Similarly, he took off his cap. The monkeys did the same. He waved his cap. The monkeys did the same. Then he threw his cap to the ground. The monkeys did nothing. The man was surprised.

Suddenly, one smart young monkey hopped down and took away the man's cap, too.

So the man yelled, "Hey, you monkeys, why didn't you throw your caps to the ground? My grandpa taught me the secret, that when I throw my cap down, you monkeys too would throw all your caps".

The smart young monkey said, "Our grandpa too taught us a secret. When the man throws his cap to the ground, be alert. Don't throw your caps or else, he will pick them up and take them away. Instead, you can take away his cap, too".

The moral of this story is, there will be hurdles. Find the solution, but remember, the same solution may not always work. Find different solutions at different times.

KEY LEARNING

Identifying the root-cause is a painful process. But, there is no shortcut to touching the root. Do not be afraid of digging.

3.5 BE PRACTICAL

Provide performance leadership through practicing examples. Experiencing is believing.

APPRECIATION

Performance management cannot be theoretical, nor is it throwing around ideas and suggestions and leaving them to others to implement. As Peter Drucker says, "ideas are cheap and abundant; what is of value is effective placement of these ideas into situations that develop into action".

While creative thinking and strategies promoting creativity need encouragement and support, no results, let alone breakthrough results, come without action. All thinking strategies should translate into action, since only action produces results.

All thinking with no action is wasteful, as is all action and no thinking. No one can succeed by instructing from a glasshouse. Preaching without practice and attention for implementation is irresponsibility.

Many managers feel they are paid to think and direct, but not to soil their hands. Unless they are personally involved, they cannot appreciate the problems in implementation. Decisions based on practical knowledge are far superior to those based purely on information. It is far better to be both decisive and action-oriented.

In every situation, there is an optimum balance between looking at too many alternatives before moving into action and not taking enough time to think about them. Successful managers have this outstanding ability to decide on where and when to draw the dividing line.

Experience has shown that, for outstanding results, quality managers should be theoretically sound and application-oriented. The data relevance, collection of the data, and its analysis may provide misleading results when not appropriately applied.

Those who emphasize only on the data and its analysis, without the knowledge of practicalities, could lead improvement teams towards disastrous results.

Ideas do not change a business, but action surely does. If one has to chose between high intelligence and effective execution, one should always prefer the latter. This is not to disparage the need for creativity and foresight, but unless it is translated into action, it is just a dream.

For instance, the data may indicate that when I first visited Pune, it rained. During my subsequent four visits also, it rained. A logical, analytical conclusion of this data is, "whenever Dr. Rau visits Pune, it rains". What a disastrous conclusion! Here, neither the data nor the analysis can be questioned. Only the lack of knowledge that there is no correlation between Dr. Rau and the rain has led to such a conclusion.

Outstanding performers continuously display brilliant energy and sparkling attitude. Organizational life is such that there are enough forces to throw lots of cold water on the performers' efforts, to keep them from staying ablaze. It is only the successful application, with its conspicuous results, that will provide unquestionable confidence in everyone around.

APPLICATION

Sajjan Singh Sarna was a successful rich businessman from the Punjab of undivided India. He was born in 1915 in Rawalpindi in a poor farmer's family and had a difficult childhood.

Having experienced poverty, innumerable hardships, and even limited education, Sajjan began eyeing the foreign shores. He stayed in Bombay and Calcutta for some time before moving to the USA. While in the States, he worked on a few odd jobs and resumed his studies.

In those days, very few Indians lived in the USA. Americans were interested in, and in fact curious about, India and Indians and invited them to address various gatherings. Sajjan too got such invitations. He liked them because his hosts would provide him with a meal and often hand over an honorarium.

One day, Sajjan was invited to talk about Indian wedding ceremonies. He worked hard to make his lecture interesting and informative. He also took with him some items that were a part of Indian wedding rituals, including small brass bells. The Americans heard him with rapt attention, and the girls in the audience were charmed by the sweet, musical, soft sound of the bells. They asked Sajjan, "Can you sell the little bells to us?"

Sajjan, of course, did sell. Sensing a great opportunity, he thought, "How about bringing the little bells into America and sell them?" He began business on the same day. He sold the bells and all the wedding ceremony items for 300 American dollars – about three thousand Rupees in those days.

Sajjan later left college and became a businessman. He would import bells from India and sell them in the USA. Slowly, his business grew to 3 million dollars per year and he became the 'Bell-King' of USA.

A poor farmer's vagabond boy became a millionaire in the USA – just because he saw an opportunity and used it.

KEY LEARNING

Performance Management is a hands-on approach. Application of this approach will ensure greater and wider acceptability with enviable results.

3.6 AVOID BUREAUCRACY

Avoid bureaucracy at all stages of management. The bigger the organization, the greater the bureaucratic justification. Corporations should realize that implementation takes place primarily at operating units. Empower them.

APPRECIATION

Large corporations need to appreciate that implementation of improved performances takes place only at their individual operating units. When they recognise its importance for achieving business objectives, these units will provide positive and vital inputs for appropriate reviews and directives from the corporate management who in turn must establish its own credibility with each unit.

While a certain degree of documentation is unavoidable at the corporate management level, too much of it defeats its very purpose. The organization should aim to avoid delays in providing mutual support and quick implementation of various initiatives, at both corporate and unit levels. The practice of treating each unit as an internal customer and exceed its expectations through structured processes and systems is often well appreciated.

The corporate management should be designed to have a committed structure with well defined responsibilities to provide direction, and to initiate, spread and facilitate various initiatives across all group companies, in order to achieve goals. It should also have the authority, though not necessarily the direct responsibility, for implementation at individual company levels. Implementation itself is best left to the individual units.

Consequently, little paperwork is required at the corporate management level. Most communication can be done one-to-one, keeping in mind consensus findings. Confrontation must be avoided, and instead, utmost respect must be accorded

All transactions must be designed and handled with the objective of not only meeting their needs, but also adding value. The corporate management must however ensure that initiatives on performance enhancement, taken at individual unit levels, are in line with the overall objectives. Any delayed action on the part of the corporate management, or working at cross purposes, will result in loss of credibility among its customers.

Experience has shown that, when one attempts to critically look at an organizational functioning, one sees several non-value added activities at each process step. Apart from decreasing the organization's compatibility, these activities firmly establish the "I create a job for you, while you do one for me" syndrome.

A good executive halts an activity if it is not entirely essential or is irrelevant or is at a point of getting obsolete. He develops the courage to say "no" to anything that is creating a bureaucratic hurdle.

An analysis made on the time spent by the senior executives of an average company showed that, on an average, only about a quarter of their time is spent on really important matters, for which they are paid. The rest of their time is fritted away on several unimportant demands on their time, which could be done by somebody else or need not be done at all.

The higher an executive goes in hierarchy, the lesser will be the proportion of his time that will be spent on real worthwhile work. It is not uncommon to find organizations whose senior executives primarily perform supervisory functions and grab all the credit.

APPLICATION

It was a hot summer day, in the year 1997, when I got a telephone call from Harsh Goenka, Chairman of RPG Enterprises. Harsh was restructuring his corporate management functions and desired to look into creating a Corporate Quality Centre. The objective was to provide a corporate framework for management of quality, as a business strategy, across the highly diversified RPG Group of Companies.

Harsh said that he came across my name as a Quality Management Consultant and was keen to have a dialogue on this initiative. On the appointed day, I went to his beautiful apartment on Carmichael Road. This first sight itself was unforgettable. I was extremely awed by the tasteful decoration of his house, with several exquisite paintings and artefacts, collected by him over years, being an avid art lover. His impeccable manners, amidst down-to-earth simplicity, impressed me instantly.

In this one-hour first meeting, he briefly dwelled upon the activities of the RP Goenka group activities, its position as the 5th largest business conglomerate in the country, the diversity of its businesses, and described how passionate he was to grow and maintain the leadership position. The group, with an annual turnover of a little over Rs.5,000 crore was on a steep growth curve and he was certain that a unified quality management initiative at the corporate was the need of the hour, which would add significant value to the group companies.

I accepted the position of Corporate Quality Advisor. Harsh was good enough to allow me the freedom to evolve my own management framework based on my earlier experiences, to suit the RPG culture. Also, he gave me direct access to him whenever I needed his intervention. His only directive was to make quality happen and ensure quality management is conspicuous across the group.

It took me about three months to visit all the group companies, numbering around thirty, interact with their CEOs and key managers and collate their inputs. It led to the evolution of the "RPG Way" for managing corporate quality and constantly integrating this initiative with the practices of the group companies. Within a twelve-month period, the corporate quality management declared the following 10 basic principles for strict compliance:

1. Recognize that Corporate Quality Management is a knowledge-based activity.
2. Carefully study the corporate culture and also the culture of individual organizations. Quality management initiatives should be in line with these cultural aspects.
3. Supplement quality initiatives at individual company levels. Avoid working at cross purpose.
4. Facilitate important projects across the corporation on a continuous basis. Avoid policing.
5. Avoid bureaucracy at corporate quality management.
6. Periodically review objectives, goals and milestones to align with the corporate vision and mission.
7. Recognize and reward team efforts on a continuous basis.
8. Manage quality only through quantification.
9. Propagate success stories through wide publicity. Success breeds success.
10. Ensure that corporate quality initiatives add value to each of the group companies.

This approach was widely appreciated across the group, and results started flowing faster than expected. Within the first year itself, there were several positive visible developments and quality management as a business strategy at RPG was getting increasingly established. Though there were several challenges during implementation, they did not prove to be unsurmountable.

Looking at the initial gains recorded by the corporate quality centre, after reviewing its performance at the board level, and in view of the forthcoming voluminous work involved, the Chairman and the Board members were unanimous that the Corporate Quality Centre, under my leadership, would be strengthened by an additional four managerial staff.

While thanking the Board for this gesture, I stuck to my declared conviction that in large corporations, quality happens at individual units and not at corporate headquarters, and there was no need to further strengthen the Centre. Thereafter, to supplement the efforts across the group, over 200 quality drivers and over 200 quality assessors and auditors were trained, covering every single unit. They, no doubt, provided invaluable support to take the quality movement forward at RPG.

Within a three-year period, there was a widespread acknowledgement that the Corporate Quality Centre was, perhaps, the most successful corporate initiative at RPG.

KEY LEARNING

Make performance management simple. It should be easy to understand and smooth to operate, with the least impediments during implementation.

3.7 REVIEW AND RESPOND

Periodically reset objectives, goals and milestones and critically review achievements against targets.

APPRECIATION

Periodic reviews, both impromptu and structured, provide immense value to the management. They are vital in many areas and are invaluable in supporting the Management Information System. Reviews help organizations ensure that all their key functions are aligned to the activities drawn up, to meet annual plans and their set goals. When such reviews are managed proactively towards improvements, both incremental and breakthrough, achieving organizational excellence would get simpler.

Review meetings should be of a definite duration with a clear agenda and should encourage total and quality participation. The Chairman should facilitate enough interaction.

Each review meeting should begins with an overview of the actions taken on the decisions of the previous meeting and should conclude with a new action plan. The plan should never be conducted in an open-ended manner, but should effectively spells out responsibilities and targeted completion dates.

Meaningful reviews bank heavily on data and quantified information. They help participants make an objective assessment of the current status and take course corrections, wherever required, for meeting individual and overall objectives. Data-based reviews are always superior to perception-based ones. Since organizations usually face many concurrent problems, it is beneficial to periodically review the progress to avoid drift and to get the focus back on key issues.

At macro-levels, reviews help in achieving the objectives set in the vision, mission and other value statements. At micro-levels, reviews help in course corrections. The frequency of reviews depends on the importance of the topics discussed and the urgency for taking corrective and preventive steps at various levels. The rule is: reviews should be as frequent as possible and should be sharply focused. Formal reviews are often provided with an agenda, either written or oral, made known to all participants in advance to enable their active contribution.

For many professionals, reviews are a pain-in-the neck. They are worried that the meetings may throw up many uncomfortable situations and, when honestly projected, they may expose wide gaps between achievements and targets. That is why laggards shy away from periodic reviews.

At review meetings, the good listeners display outstanding managerial skills. A good listener is always a better decision-maker. In present times, top executives spend over two-thirds of their time in meetings, listening to others and participating in discussions. This is quite tiring and exhausting, and sometimes boring, and for making any meaningful decision, he or she has to be a great listener.

As John Maxwell said, "smart leaders believe only half of what they hear. Discerning leaders know which half to believe". Each top executive has his own style of increasing comprehension of what is being said, so that at the end of such meetings, he can aptly add his punch lines with definite finality.

APPLICATION

Bill Gates, 51, will step away from his daily role as chief software architect of Microsoft in the Summer of 2008 to focus on the work of his Foundation. The Gates Foundation, set up in 1994, has so far given away about $11 billion. In the next three years, it will be granting about $3 billion every year.

In 2005, according to the Foundation Centre of United States, only 15 private foundations in the USA had assets of $3 billion and above.

"We're giving over a billion and half dollars today, so it's not starting from scratch," said Gates, who visited Silicon Valley in the middle of November 2006 to receive the James C. Morgan Global Humanitarian Award from the Tech Museum in San Jose. "This is doubling in three years. Although it is different from business, since Microsoft more than doubled in less than three years several times, some of these things about scaling up and all that are familiar to Patty Stonesifer (CEO of the Foundation), Melinda Gates and myself."

Though Gates' vision extends around the world, his giving away began with the United Way. His parents, long supporters of the agency that funds multiple social service non-profits, inspired his philanthropy.

In 1999, when United Way Silicon Valley faced financial crisis, Gates helped by writing a $5 million cheque. Today, he encourages his employees to donate, as well. Microsoft, which matches up to $12,000 per employee each year, is one of the most generous supporters of United Way Silicon Valley. In the year 2005, the company and its employees in Mountain View contributed more than $1 million to the agency.

The bulk of Gate's philanthropic effort is focused on education and global health. Last year, the Foundation distributed grants of more than $284 million to schools and educational projects, and more than $844 million to health initiatives, the area that triggers the most passion in Gates.

"This is the biggest priority at our Foundation: the way that human life is not treated equitably between rich countries and poor countries", he said.

The size and potential of the Gates Foundation stirs awe - and concern - in the philanthropy world. The Gates Foundation will soon represent about 10 per cent of America's total private foundation assets, and that worries Bruce Sievers, a visiting scholar at Stanford University and former executive director of the Walter and Elise Hass Fund in San Francisco. "That's a lot of power in the hands of a small group", he said. "They have the potential to set a social agenda for society", Sievers added.

When quizzed on the parallels between his work as a global philanthropist and the work at Microsoft, Gates replied, "they are identical in a lot of ways. It's about picking smart people who want to dedicate themselves to the problem, taking a long-term approach, being willing to have some failures and come back around and learn from those things. The paradigm of how we plan, how we pull the team together is virtually the same, and it is partly why the Foundation has come on to the diseases like malaria, which kills a million people a year. We have been able to galvanize a lot of activity very quickly."

KEY LEARNING

Reviews provide the required direction to ensure continual improvements important to the health of the organization.

3.8 ENCOURAGE TEAM PARTICIPATION

Make every employee of your organization participative. Be simple in your dealings. Do not confuse with jargons.

APPRECIATION

Organizational performance, though often driven by a visionary at the top, is a product of collective effort. Each employee, however, low he may be placed on an organizational hierarchy, has a job to perform. He or she contributes whenever the participation level is high. It is essential for organizations to continuously empower each of their employees. Training, hand-holding, honest feedback, counselling and appreciation of good work are some of the methods that enable such an empowerment.

Remember that whenever team meetings take place, there are only a few members who are more vocal. We should not allow one or two persons to highjack the meetings. For team efforts to succeed, managements should discourage improvement or problem-solving teams who are not participative.

Apart from enhancing performance confidence, a total participation also draws out a sense of ownership from each member. When team participation is given due importance, members will fearlessly comment on the both the positive and negative progress of the project. They will be highly communicative, even when there are discouraging results, once they perceive team-members as equal.

Dr. A.P.J. Abdul Kalam speaks of igniting young minds of India so that India can turn into a developed nation by 2020. He says, all through his career in the field of technology and its management, he relied heavily on the power and potential of youth. "My strength has been my young teams who never let me down", he says. Through his projects in space, defence and nuclear sectors, Dr. Kalam knows that Indians have the ability to achieve the best in the world.

According to Kalam, "We need to adapt implementation of our programmes and policies into a mission mode to succeed. Our abundant national resources, human and material, remain to be fully utilized."

The key is human resource. The measure of success of a leader is how he crafts utilizing all those under his command, and not only by the problems he successfully tackles but also by those he helps to solve. He is one who recognizes that the problems do not recur because those at the operating levels are involved in solving them while taking ownership for their further non-occurrence.

There is a huge difference between groups and teams. It is the groups of people who attend public functions and politicians' meetings, while it is the teams who participate in competitive games. Teams synergize each one's efforts towards a significant benefit. Synergizing means: two plus two is not four, but twenty-two. The team-members work together cooperatively towards a well-defined objective, add value to one another, make decisions through consensus and are jointly responsible for the outcome.

Teams' performances go beyond expectations when its members are continuously trained in handling the latest tools and techniques. Further, they love to be convinced that they are being fully supported. In the final analysis, the one quality that all successful leaders have is the ability to take on responsibility. As John Maxwell said, "a leader can give up anything – except final responsibility".

APPLICATION

One fine morning, a pigeon was flying low through a jungle, his eyes scanning the ground for a good breakfast. Soon, he spotted rice and wheat grains strewn on a beautiful green patch.

"What a delicious breakfast!" the pigeon exclaimed, landed smoothly and started eating away the luscious food. After the hearty self-serving, he flapped his wings, ready to take-off when, to his surprise, he found his feet entangled in a net. The realisation dawned on him: a bird catcher had spread a net and had strewn grains over it. The trapped pigeon looked around, sad and not knowing how to free himself.

A few moments later, another pigeon started descending for the 'breakfast'. The first pigeon shouted to warn his friend, but it was too late. The grains were sweeter than the shouts. The second pigeon was caught too.

They were followed by the third, the fourth, the fifth and so on, the whole green patch was covered by twenty to thirty pigeons caught in the net, all lamenting their fate. They knew the bird catcher would soon appear and take them in cages, to be sold in the market.

Then a young pigeon told the others that he had a mouse friend who lived near the river. If the mouse was here, it could cut away the net and they could all be free. But,

"Oh," said another pigeon, "if one of us could fly to the river to the friend and call him here."

Suddenly, a wise old pigeon said, "let us do one thing. Why don't we try to fly together?"

"Yes, yes", all agreed. So the wise leader said, "when I call one-two-three, all of us should take-off simultaneously". "Yes, yes", all said in a chorus.

And so, they all flew away as one big bird, with the net still entangled to their and landed happily at the river. Soon, the mouse set them free.

KEY LEARNING

Remember teams are different from groups.Teams invariably synergize.

3.9 TELL A STORY

Never carry irrelevant stories, whether real or imaginary. They are counterproductive and can sometimes be detrimental to performance movement.

APPRECIATION

It is highly beneficial to relate most things, especially past performance, through stories, more so when organizational communications are tough and participants are stiff. Recalling stories of both successes and failures get wider acceptance when they are in alignment with the current situation.

Several stories get evolved while going along any improvement journey. They need to be appropriately moderated to make them useful and must be impersonal, interesting, educative, relevant to the management approach, and add value to the process steps.

However, one often comes across cases where individuals or situations are pushed on to the frontline and stories are created around them. The stories are then not impersonal, but are personality-oriented. Such stories are damaging to performance enhancement of any organization. Cut short such stories early. Senior management boards have a major role to play to discourage such a tendency.

Every leader must realize that the power to motivate followers rests almost solely on the ability to communicate and participate effectively. In most business situations, a private one-to-one conversation is much more effective than an open talk.

A contemporary leader who is an introvert and shy (as Lincoln was in his youth) must make every effort to overcome this trait. A person with a great deal of talent must also be capable of expressing himself.

It is sad that a large number of managers, even today, do not communicate well. They are highly self-centred, protective, secretive, and hold information as if it were their personal property. When they communicate, the attempts are *ad hoc* and lack conviction, and their results are often very different from what are hoped for. As a result, misunderstanding, confusion, mistrust and conflict thrive in their organizations at all levels. Employees do not get a free flow of information, leading to irrelevant ideas and inadequate actions that would make them unproductive.

Leading managements ensure appropriate deployment of every single aspect impacting performances at all levels. To make it happen, they realize communication is the key. They make sure that such communication is effective, and constantly measure the effectiveness.

Some stories could be quite damaging. Employees often relate themselves to the top man, and are eager to pass on to him what he wants to hear and not what he should hear. When that happens, the organization is the loser. Proximity to the power is the winner, along with those who play such games. They would soon emerge as the sought-after story tellers, leading to organizational sickness.

Problems will continue to mount and their consequences will badly impact the organizational performance. Even trivial problems, which can be easily nipped in the bud, will later turn out to be significant ones, taking everyone by surprise. By the time the management wakes up, the damage will already be done. Leading organizations discourage such damaging stories.

People do matter in any organization. They are involved in a complex and ever-changing web of social interactions, relationships at home and professional challenges on the job. The complexity may be short-lived and transitory or longlasting, severely impacting their behaviour towards themselves and towards everyone around. They may then completely switch themselves off, get irritated, be rude to, be angry with, be indifferent to everyone around.

How do enlightened managements get over such uncomfortable situations? They tell stories that are relevant, significant and situation-friendly.

APPLICATION

By the time Abraham Lincoln took office of President of United States of America, seven states had seceded from the union to form the Confederate States of America. Barely ten days before he took the oath on 4th March, 1861, Jefferson Davis was sworn in as president of the Confederacy in Montgomery, Alabama.

There were rumours that Lincoln's inauguration would be disrupted, the president killed, and the city taken by Confederates. The nation's capital was, in fact, placed under armed alert. In the midst of all this turmoil, a relatively unknown Abraham Lincoln took the oath as the nation's sixteenth president. He was the first Republican president, elected by a minority of the popular vote. By the end of his four-year rule, Lincoln proved to be a man who really knew how to lead the country and demonstrated several leadership qualities and abilities that saved the nation.

Lincoln often influenced people through storytelling. In a letter to one of his friends he explained, "they say I tell a great many stories. I reckon I do, but I have learnt from long experience that simple people are more easily influenced through the medium of a broad and humourous illustration than in any other way".

He could talk with ease to anyone – brilliant scientist, wily politician, visiting head of state, or simple backwoods farmer. He had a terrific sense of humour, often sprinkling his conversations with witty stories and humourous anecdotes that he used as his persuasive tools. He had come to be regarded as the only President of the United States who was a true humourist.

He enjoyed talking to people, which was one reason he created such open access to the White House. During his presidency, everyone and anyone was invited to come in and talk to him.

As a matter of fact, nearly every person who came in contact with this sixteenth President was amazed at the huge inventory of anecdotes, jokes and stories. Furthermore, he possessed the ability to instantly pull out just the right one for any occasion that may arise. Lincoln was a master at the art of storytelling, and he used that ability purposefully and effectively during his dealings as President of the United States.

People were fascinated by his wit and hilarity and, as a result, many of his anecdotes found their way into print while he was still alive. In fact, hundreds of other stories were attributed to Lincoln which he himself had never even heard of.

During his years in the White House, Lincoln's storytelling became so legendary that amusing stories started to circulate about him. One that he was fond of, involving himself, was about two Quaker women in a railway coach who were overheard in a conversation:

"I think Jefferson will succeed", said the first.

"Why do you think so?" asked the second.

"Because Jefferson is a praying man."

"And so is Abraham a praying man."

"Yes, but the Lord will think Abraham is joking."

KEY LEARNING

Storytelling is not restricted to babies. It is a useful tool in enlightening performance enhancement teams.

3.10 UNDERSTANDING SUBTLE DIFFERENCES

Appreciate the subtle difference between groups and teams.

APPRECIATION

Remember that it is groups of people who attend social events, public meetings, parties, annual gatherings, etc. They do so after being informed, or even invited. They derive personal satisfaction in attending these one-off events. Their attendance has a limited purpose: be a part of a celebration, or enjoy a concert, or listen to an enlightened speaker and try grasping some wisdom. Groups have little bonding within themselves or with others. The members are essentially individualistic.

On the other hand, teams are change agents and team-members contribute and complement each other. They work together with a common objective. Each team-member has an important task, or a set of tasks, to perform. Their performances are often measured, critically reviewed and continuously improved. Members of a team invariably address all the three vital components of performance excellence, namely, ability, attitude and application.

Teams are adequately trained and encouraged to apply the learning. Each team-member is equipped with necessary softer skills to supplement competence in his job. The senior management continues to provide adequate opportunities to apply and demonstrate their capabilities for organizational benefit.

Though the common belief is that most people resist change, very few of them would like to work in an organization that is static. Being a part of the dynamics of change excite several individuals. Being change agents, they welcome change since it brings them a sense of continual achievement and excitement.

It is unlikely that every team-member is enthusiastically receptive to change. We always find some who are averse to risk, and may not be so participative in the team process. Only rarely, reactions of these individuals will frustrate leading managements.

Most forms of incremental change cause no resistance at all, more so when they are perceived as a part of the job. Problems crop up when additional tasks are added, requiring a new mind set. A paradigm shift, therefore, invites maximum resistance.

For enlightened organizations, breakthrough thoughts, breakthrough actions and breakthrough results are a part of their culture. Fundamental change is an important component of their game plan, made visible and understood by one and all, by making the implications understood by all functions. They can be managed successfully only through participation of all employees in this dynamically changing process and through building team relationships.

Most team efforts are unwritten contracts. The members develop tremendous softer skills like participating and communicating, as well as presentation skills, and enjoy sharpening them as their companionship improves.

For teams to succeed, participation is the key. Being a part of a team-member, one gets involved in identifying with the likely benefits and ensures that they are real. Participation helps reduce resistance to change in many situations. It can create ownership to encourage implementing the proposed change through creating better awareness of the change, and the reasons for it.

APPLICATION

Look at the culinary habits of housewives.

The other day, we had a dinner invitation from Subba Rao's family. Though Indian joint families are an obsolete part of culture, it was great to see four generations happily living together in his house, sharing both pain and pleasure. We were introduced to the eldest in the family, an octogenarian, her daughter, grand daughter, and the great grand kids.

Having reached the house early in the evening, we sat around for a couple of hours recalling the past of each of the generations. There were so many stories because each one had several experiences to share. As expected, the stories from the eldest lady were the most hilarious.

At the dining table, while food was being served, one could not resist asking who had taken so much trouble to prepare so many delicious dishes. The quick answer was, as per the normal practice, each one had shared in the burden.

At the end of the seven-course dinner, everyone unanimously agreed the food was delicious. Subba Rao and his family members were profusely thanked for hosting the event and for making the evening so delightful.

Just before leaving the house, everyone was invited to participate in an interesting game. Each guest was asked to rank the items on the seven-course dinner in the order of increasing taste. Initially, there was reluctance to participate, since such a grading might hurt someone or the other in the household. However, the family assured the guests that there would not be any ill-feelings among them and it was meant to be a fun game.

The results were fascinating. The tastiest dishes were those prepared by the oldest in the house. When everyone was appreciating the "winner", a young child of the household commented that whatever grandma made, she made with a lot of passion. "She puts in that little extra effort", she said, "though every other person in the family is also committed to perform".

KEY LEARNING

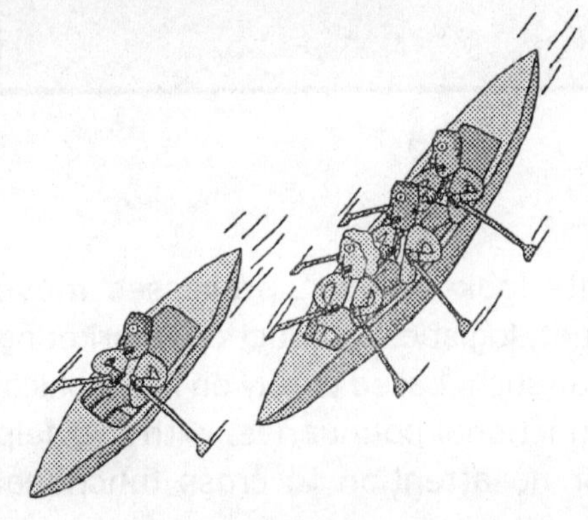

Recognise differences between seeing and observing, reading and studying, and facts and perceptions. Only successful teams can distinguish these subtle, and yet significant, differences.

3.11 INVOLVE ONE AND ALL

Involve every single employee. One weak link in a process-step is sufficient to snap the process chain.

APPRECIATION

While departmental hierarchical managements look vertical, processes move horizontal. Each department, whether it is procurement, logistics, production, marketing or any other, tends to operate in silos and is managed as such, based purely on hierarchical approach. It tries to be efficient within its routine, functional boundaries, with the help of age-old vertical reporting system, with little or no attention to cross functional needs.

Hierarchical managements do not pose major problems in companies but are totally inadequate. Leader organizations recognize that fact. Reporting relationships ensure necessary discipline between senior employees and subordinates and their involvement, since interaction between them is continuously appraised for its effectiveness.

Further, hierarchical seniority gives management control on juniors, through identification and implementation of rewards and punishments.

Processes do not follow vertical hierarchical path. They move parallel horizontally. They interface with more than one department and function, as a chain of functional steps, which convert an input into an output. Each process has several process steps and interfaces between process-steps can create weak links that make performance unsatisfactory. Each of the employees performs two vital roles, both as a customer and as a supplier. He is a customer to the previous process step and supplier to the next one.

Thus, each one has a dual role to perform. It is only the internalization of customer–supplier relationship that would focus on this approach and produce excellent results.

It is hard to find consistent results only through hierarchical management. This is more prominent in large organizations where employees' commitment and involvement in cross-functional relationships is lukewarm. Since the organization as a whole is accountable to performances that meet its final customers, both in products and services, it is necessary to recognize that each process chain has many links, and everyone who has a responsibility in the chain and its links should not only get totally involved, but also take ownership in deliverables.

Managements should proactively involve in promoting cross-functional relationships, and reward and recognize those who enhance such relationships.

Global organizations extend this cross-functional relationship through involvement of all stakeholders. The customer and supplier meetings, periodically organized to get the pulse on the quality perceptions on their relationship, provide valuable inputs and at the same time give these stakeholders the confidence that they are being treated as an extended arm of the organization. Their honest feedback and contribution could be of immense value for achieving enhanced performances.

Involving those outside the organization will be futile if there is inadequacy in the excited involvement of the employees. External stakeholders do not hesitate to actively participate when they are assured of total involvement of employees at all levels.

APPLICATION

Near a river in a jungle lived two good friends, a pigeon and an ant. As soon as the sun would rise, the two friends would come out and greet each other. They would then have breakfast, play around, sing and dance. Life was wonderful with happiness abound.

One night, the river started flowing with fury and the whole jungle was flooded. The water rushed into the ant's home, and it started screaming for help, louder and louder each passing moment.

The pigeon had his nest on one of the branches of a large tree nearby. The ant's screams woke him up. The pigeon saw the flood and realised the gravity of the situation. He immediately picked up a dry leaf in his beak and flew to the ant. "Dear friend Ant, please sit on the leaf", he called out. As soon as the ant crawled onto the leaf, the pigeon picked up the leaf again.

He flew far away from the river and set the leaf down on a tree. The ant crawled off the leaf – he was safe! He thanked the pigeon profusely. The two friends then made new homes at the new place and lived happily there., enjoying great meals, the sun, singing, dancing and everything.

Several days later, the pigeon invited his friend ant for breakfast at his home. To save the ant the trouble of climbing to his home, the pigeon picked him up on a leaf. The two had a good breakfast and were relaxing with sweet dialogue.

Suddenly, the ant bit the pigeon on his foot. The startled pigeon jumped up in pain and anger and flew away. A loud gunshot followed almost immediately. The pigeon circled in the sky for a few moments and then returned. He was still very angry and began scolding the ant for biting him. "You are ungrateful", he shouted.

The ant then pointed to a man walking away from the tree and said, "Look there. He is a hunter. He had come to hunt a bird and was aiming at you. You did not see him but I did. I bit you so that you would fly away and avoid getting killed".

"Thank you, dear friend", said the pigeon gratefully. Then the two had a hearty laugh.

KEY LEARNING

Develop camaraderie among stakeholders. That ensures sterling performance.

3.12 SHOW HOW

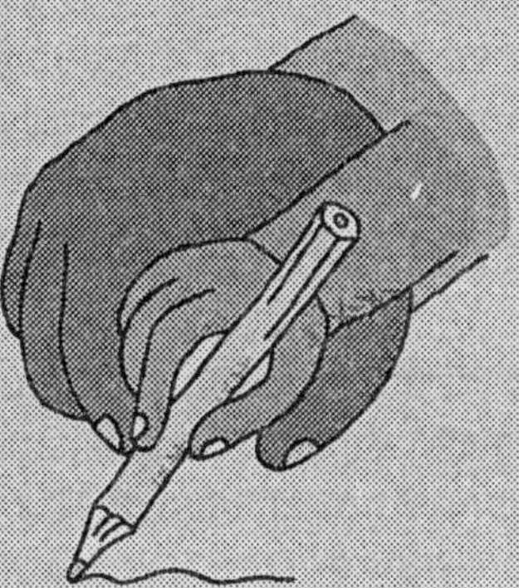

To ensure outstanding success, facilitation through 'show-how' is the key. Handheld projects invariably prove to be highly successful.

APPRECIATION

Facilitation is a knowledge-based activity and facilitators, as enablers for improved performance, are knowledge workers. They are highly respected, actively contribute, easy to get along, openly communicate, positively involve without interference, and are in a position to continuously infuse new ideas that add value at every process step addressed by them.

Several facilitators know how to do things, are very strong in theory and have much information at their disposal. With the advancement of information technology, one can have access through the internet to a large quantum of information on every subject under the sun. They tend to collate the information, articulate the same – some with curiously sounding jargon – and deliver it as a knowledge pack. But, when challenged to demonstrate its usefulness or effectiveness, they miserably fail.

Persons with great presentation skills, without any application competence, may appear initially impressive, and sail through. But, their limited competencies will be exposed when faced with live situations where they need to apply their inputs. Information-based facilitation has several inadequacies and cannot lead to sustained improvements.

Attention to only knowledge-based activity, with little application ensures only partial results. This is particularly true when a knowledge-based approach leads to only theoretical inputs, without the necessary practical and applicability aspects.

Successful application is therefore the key to become a knowledge worker. Anyone can read literature and understand how to swim. But, to become even a simple swimmer, forget about ace championship, one has to practice swimming. The same is true about cooking. You cannot hope to become a great cook just by reading books on cookery several times. Similarly, the airline ticketing personnel gets more efficient only after she has handled an increasingly large number of passengers.

Information gets converted into knowledge only when it is applied. It is a judicious mix of theory and practice that helps one to become increasingly knowledgeable. That would enhance the show–how competence, which is appreciated by all levels of an organization, covering both line and staff functions. These functions are quick to recognize the importance of handholding inputs, particularly when they supplement the initiatives already taken at the operational levels.

Management efforts do register greater success if the know-how inputs are supplemented with a 'show-how' approach, that is immediately applied. Such an approach surely enhances credibility, resulting in improved participation at all levels. The result, then, is an outcome of combined effort, and is easily demonstrated. Whenever facilitators handhold and mix with employees, irrespective of their hierarchical positions, everyone applauds. They, then, become an integral part of networking for continuous improvement. Show-how facilitators are not afraid of roadblocks. They squarely face them and remove the impediments with lasting success.

Show-how is handholding and not spoonfeeding.

APPLICATION

One day in Madras, some students were debating over some words of English. When the debate led to heated arguments with no conclusion, the students went to Prof. Jones, a scholar in the English language. But, Prof. Jones too was confused. He had never considered those words. He could not explain clearly, though he uttered something, and sent the students away.

There was a clever, intelligent and hardworking boy who was not present during the debate. The debating students sought his help. The boy did not immediately respond, but headed straightaway for the library. For many hours, he scanned through several books, studied some up to mid-night and even borrowed a bunch for further study at home.

The next morning, the boy expounded to his friends on the origin of the words, their history, meaning, usage, etc. When he met Prof. Jones and shared his findings, the Professor embraced the clever boy. He later suggested, "Write an essay on this subject and we will print it in the college magazine". The boy was elated and wrote the essay that was published, read and appreciated by one and all.

Lord Raleigh, a professor in English and author of several books on the subject, also read the essay and was extremely impressed by its brilliance. He later wrote a congratulatory letter to the boy.

The boy grew up to be a scholar in the English language and also in Physics. He solved many intricate problems in physics and made many discoveries. Later, he was awarded the Nobel Prize for Physics.

That boy was Sir C V Raman.

KEY LEARNING

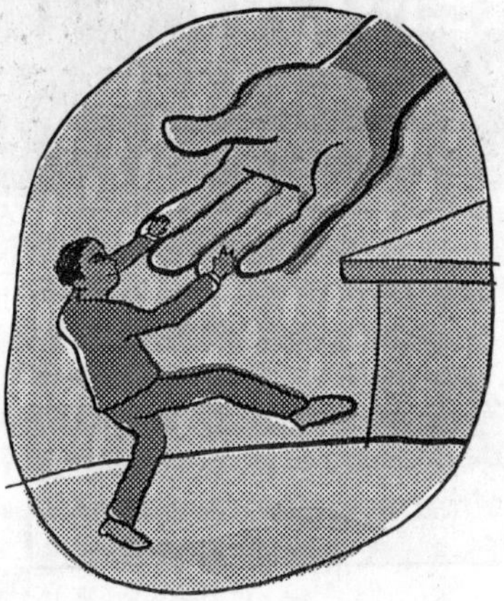

Know-how has only a limited appreciation. It is the 'show-how' that carries conviction.

4

Chapter

FOCUS ON MEASUREMENT

Perceptive managements are deceptive.
Measurable managements ensure sustainable performances.

CONTENTS

4.1 ONLY FACTS

Facts, facts and facts.
Avoid gut-feeling.

APPRECIATION

The management board of any large corporation, at the apex level, encourages its group companies to formulate their own operational policies for business, within the overall framework of the group.

Each CEO manages the company as he or she deems fit, keeping in mind corporate expectations, customers' needs and business realities. There is often, relatively less day-to-day control from the corporate. Review meetings address performances against targets, and study the trends against the plans. To that extent, deployment from corporate level is limited to policy communication from the top level, reviews at macro-levels and support to lower levels, wherever necessary.

Corporations should realize that, while individual companies operate with a high degree of freedom and focus on specific operational targets, they also need a common corporate thread to intertwine, to maintain a single corporate identity. The declared value statements, including corporate vision and mission statements, indeed help in providing the units a direction to declare their own operational values and align them to corporate values.

Unity in diversity is the biggest challenge for corporate quality management. There are three specific issues that achieve this integration:

1. Appreciation of corporate business and corporate quality objectives;

2. Alignment to individual company's interests; and

3. Integration through proactive approaches such as continuous facilitation, quarterly reviews for continuous improvement, periodic workshops to enhance employee skills, an in-house quality magazine aimed at spreading success stories with a relatively high degree of internal and external focus.

Fact-based management, rather than gut feeling or whimsical approach, needs to be encouraged at every stage. Even in those cases where decisions are taken without quantification, appropriate facts should be collected quickly to validate the decision already taken. Fact-based decision-making is a powerful tool and is always more reliable, provided the facts are facts.

While facts and figures can be powerful, they can also be boring. Numbers by themselves do not present a complete story. When you see them, use them appropriately and judiciously. Bring them alive. Incorporate facts and figures that are live and really interesting. Stories involving people and events make facts sound fascinating.

"The main part of intellectual education is not the acquisition of facts, but is learning how to make facts live", according to Oliver Wendell Holmes, an American Judge. Medical practice is a classic example of how facts are made alive, and effectively used.

While deliberating on facts, the importance of segmentation cannot be overlooked. Studies have proved that the most supporting aids for top management are process differentiation, process development and innovation. While resorting to such segmentation, it is essential to give attention to fact-based logic. Several other studies have reiterated that fact-based segment management is an easier path towards enhancement in financial performance.

Management by facts requires a number of measurements that are derived from the organization's needs and strategy, and should provide critical data and information about key processes and results. Performance measurements usually focus on input data, environmental data, processing data, cost data and output data and their measurement system.

Apart from the fact-based management related to operations, which many leading companies adopt, prosperous organizations are internally evolving consistent frameworks for measuring other key dimensions, such as vision, mission, core values like integrity, humility, tolerance and responsibility, contribution to both long and short-term perspectives, and commitment to both knowledge and information systems.

APPLICATION

Sometime last year, I was amused while reading the following news item in the *Business Line,* the financial daily from the Hindu Group of Publications under the caption: *Andhra Pradesh Government firm on completing irrigation projects*:

"The state government is determined to complete long-pending irrigation projects such as the Polavaram project and all avenues will be explored to find the requisite resources, said Dr. Y. S. Rajasekhara Reddy, chief minister.

He spoke at a number of public meetings in the East Godavari district on Sunday, touring villages as a part of 'Rajiv Palle Baata' programme.

He said that he would lay the foundation stone for the work on the Polavaram Right Canal project in West Godavari district on Monday. It would be named after former Prime Minister Indira Gandhi.

Dr. Reddy also said that the Polavaram project would be a great boon to both East and West Godavari districts and the north coastal districts of Visakhapatnam, Vizainagaram and Srikakulam.

'The Polavaram project will fulfil the long-cherished desire of the people of north coastal and Godavari districts', Dr. Reddy said.

Besides, the project would facilitate transfer of Godavari water to the Krishna basin to stabilise the Krishna delta. Nearly 1,000mw of power would also be generated.

The project is estimated to cost over Rs. 8,000 crore.

Some 25 years ago, "T. Anjayya, the then Congress chief minister, laid the foundation stone for the project and subsequently, N. T. Rama Rao, the Telugu Desam chief minister, also did the same. Dr. Reddy was the third chief minister to do so."

Facts, facts and facts from Indian politicians!!!

KEY LEARNING

Fact-based management is indeed a powerful management tool, if honestly applied.

4.2 LEARN TO QUANTIFY

Manage quality only through quantification. Remember that every single quality attribute is quantifiable.

APPRECIATION

With Total Quality Management (TQM) methodologies well developed, the art and science of quality management discourages the management of quality without quantification. Whether it is an incremental quality improvement or a breakthrough quality enhancement, the objective should be to clearly spell out the current levels of quality, set targets for improvement or enhancement levels, based on the customers' needs, and quantify the gaps to be bridged in clear terms.

There has been a paradigm shift in defining, understanding, appreciating and managing quality. Quality is no more restricted to the final product or service quality. It includes all processes, all systems, documentation, delivery and, in fact, every single commitment made to both internal and external customers. Above all, quality includes cost. The higher the quality, the lower is the cost. It is only when a product has additional features — like a television set — does it cost more, and not because it works better. Quality is conformity to commitment at every step in the company's operations, thereby avoiding expensive rework and scrap.

Further, quality is no more qualitative. Every single attribute, including beauty, attitude, commitment and behaviour are quantifiable and managed through quantification.

While arriving at such quantitative improvements, based on the customer needs, the process capability component cannot be overlooked. Aiming at quality improvements which are not within the capabilities of existing processes, current systems and prevailing employee responses may lead to disastrous consequences. When the present capabilities are defined and desired gaps are quantified, it is easy for the management to decide on the new technological inputs to be pumped in to meet customers' increasing quality demands.

While working on quality enhancement through improvement projects, organizations often set intermediate milestones to be achieved to reach the final objectives. Milestones are created only through a systematic approach, and are quantified, so that they can be monitored during reviews.

Improvement projects at a large Indian group, RPG Enterprises – there are about three thousand successful projects over a five-year period – present problem-definition in sharply quantified terms as the first step. The definitions are invariably quantified and are within the measurement competence of the organization. RPG's philosophy is that every quality attribute is quantifiable, anything that is quantifiable is measurable, anything that is measurable is monitorable, and anything that is monitorable is manageable.

At RPG, the quantified benefits derived through implementation are reviewed against the targets with definite periodicity, at both corporate and company levels.

Several types of data and information are needed for performance measurement and enhancement. They need to be relevant, authentic and their integrity never in doubt. The data and information should be adequate for a meaningful analysis. Analysis refers to extracting significant meaning from the data and information that would provide support to process-evaluation, decision-making and operational-improvement.

A major consideration towards performance improvement and change management is the selection and use of the right type of performance measures or indicators. The selected ones should best represent the factors that throw up during the improvement process. Though the tracking process, if required, these measures or indicators themselves may need refinement.

APPLICATION

Let us challenge the way we think about numbers by looking at this tricky puzzle:

Mr. Greenwich and his wife, Mrs. Greenwich from London were shopping in a mall one day when they realised they were very much behind schedule. Since each one had separate shopping lists, they decided to shop on their own.. As the converging point, they agreed to meet at their bank at 2 p.m.

Several minutes later, Mr. Greenwich was through with his list and looked at his wrist for the time and realised he had forgotten to wear his watch. He asked a lady walking by for the correct time. Her watch was 5 minutes fast, but she thought it was 10 minutes slow.

Mrs. Greenwich too had left her watch at home, so she asked a gentleman passing by for the correct time. The man's watch was 10 minutes slow, but he thought it was 15 minutes fast.

Taking into account the errors in the watches, who was at the bank first and at what time did each arrive?

The answer may initially puzzle. Mr. Greenwich arrived first at 1:45 p.m. He had been told a time that was actually 15 minutes faster than the true time. Mrs. Greenwich arrived 25 minutes after the hour, that is, at 2:25 p.m., since she had been told a time that was 25 minutes slower than the true time.

KEY LEARNING

Every quality attribute is quantifiable.

4.3 VALUE CUSTOMER VOICE

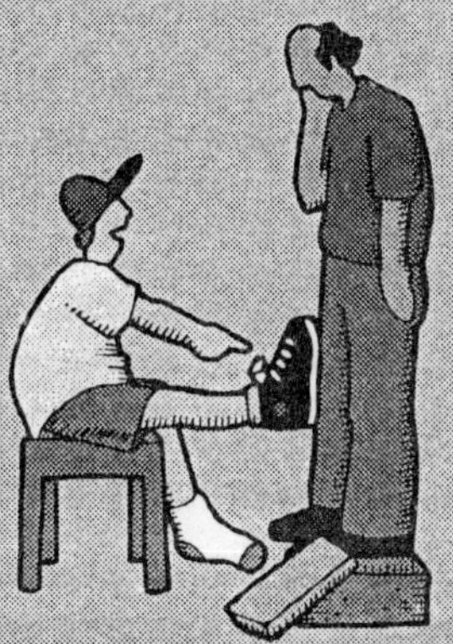

Internalize customer-supplier relationship. It is a powerful tool for performance enhancement by networking through process steps.

APPRECIATION

Every single management effort is customer-driven and process-centric. Customers, who receive the output of a process could be internal or external or both. The voice of the customer leads to issues that are critical to the quality of the processes. Advanced quality management techniques are increasingly focusing on the voice of the customer to arrive at measurable requirements that are critical to quality, and integrating them with the **voice** of the processes.

The voice of the customer may not always provide quantified input. It could also be stated in general terms and even qualitative terms. Typical voices could be like: 'we want you to be our preferred supplier', 'we need your commercial proposal immediately', 'we need you to respond quickly', 'we want you to ensure information security', and 'we are not comfortable with your product and your service'.

Quality improvement teams have to necessarily move on to convert these qualitative voices to specific, measurable, actionable and manageable terms. These terms, which are critical to quality, help them to know exactly what product features or process performance levels are required, in order to meet the customers' needs. Focused management of the voice of the customer ensures that your customers are continuously assured of your intentions and actions.

Customers would love when they are handled the way they want you to handle them. Building customer loyalty is, thankfully, not an art, neither a rocket science. It doesn't depend on any mathematical formula, nor does it necessarily require total re-engineering. It's just focusing on your customers, making them feel that you really know them and are indeed listening to them and you are there to create 'cliff hangers' that intrigue them.

Leading organizations give adequate importance to not only activity-networking, but also to quality-networking at every process step, by appreciating that, in any supply-chain, there are several internal customers and suppliers in every activity. When this thought is implemented, the internal 'customer-supplier' relationship gets strengthened. Every employee recognises that he has a dual role to play: namely, a customer to the previous step and a supplier to the next step. Employee competences, to meeting both the quantity and the quality needs of a process step get built on this thought.

When all employees ensure desired performances at these dual roles, the quality at each process step will be in line with the designed outcome. The final outcome will be in line with the product and service specification, driven by the customers' voice.

Many leading companies realise that the production of the best products, and servicing them on time, are necessary but not sufficient. The deliverables need to get customized for each customer, in order to become the choice supplier. Product specifications need to become customer–centric, covering packaging and delivery systems as well. The companies then look at those attributes that core customers value the most, where the companies can score well.

The voice of the customer is being heard through direct communication, with a free flow of information that allows organization experts from both sides to resolve problems related to product quality, deficiencies in distribution and quick, efficient delivery. Seeking customer voice proactively not only shortens the lines of such communication but also helps in promoting a sense of ownership in evolving solutions to the problems.

Currently, there is a new trend of capturing the voice of the customer. Many service organizations, particularly the financial institutions, banks and telecom service providers are trying to get the customer voice through mobile phones, calling both existing and potential customers indiscriminately. With highly sophisticated technology on hand, they are attempting to capture the customer voice through this impersonal method, which is resented even by genuine customers.

Even with the application of the state-of-the-art technologies, the best practices in meeting customer expectations ultimately revert to the people behind these machines — the employees who meet customers face-to-face, attend to their needs, and swiftly deal with their problems. They are in the best position to capture and interpret customer voices, and galvanize the entire organization to be customer-centric.

APPLICATION

It was the year 2003. I had just landed at the international wing of Mumbai airport, after a gruelling travel from Jakarta, Indonesia where I spent four days leading a team to assess quality practices of an outstanding cotton yarn plant, PT Elegant Textiles, one of the several companies of Aditya Birla Group. Elegant Textiles had applied to compete for the President's Platinum Award, the highest in-house recognition for excellent overall performance.

When the flight landed, it was nearly 3 a.m. Immigration clearance and custom formalities were unexpectedly smooth. Being a frequent traveller, I was amazed at how the government authorities have improved their efficiency and their traveller-friendliness.

Then, when I walked into the luggage-claim enclosure, the problems began. No luggage trolleys were at hand. The available few were picked up by some passengers from the earlier flights. I learnt that five international flights had landed simultaneously—hence the chaos. Thirty minutes later, I finally grabbed one trolley and rushed to the luggage belt, surrounded by hundreds of passengers eagerly awaiting their luggage.

I could pick up my luggage after another 35 minutes' wait. I waited for a further 15 minutes for my driver. He did not bring my car to the airport at the scheduled time, and I learnt that he could not make it due to some personal problem. So, I settled for a pre-paid taxi to take me home, about 20 minutes' drive on an early morning.

The car, a 1995 vintage Fiat was painted black and yellow, as per the Mumbai Road Transport Office rules. In a bid to be environment-friendly and to drastically bring down fuel costs, it ran on Natural Gas. The car was originally designed for petrol fuel, but having been converted to the environment-friendly natural gas, the only place to fix the LPG cylinder was the car boot, taking over much of the luggage space. Now, there was place for only one bag! The other three were adjusted in the front seat.

When I entered the cab, I was annoyed with the little leg room in the back seat. The front seat was pushed back to provide total comfort to the driver. In fact, the back doors could not be fully opened, and it was a task manoeuvring oneself inside.

The good Sardarji driver, noticed my difficulty, but was the least sympathetic. Instead, he commented that probably I had not used the Mumbai taxi for a long time. The only consolation was his assurance that he would drive me to my home within 20 minutes, instead of the normal 30 minutes.

Once he started accelerating, everything in the taxi began rattling. No part of the vehicle seemed to be adequately tightened. Moreover, his driving was so rough, it was too frightening for comfort. Curiously, I glanced at the dashboard. All meters were in place, but none of them seemed to be working. I was certain he had his own way of determining the level of gas, oil position in the engine, speed and even battery condition.

After sometime, I could not contain my curiosity and asked him how he could drive his taxi without any of the instruments functioning. His was a matter-of-fact reply: "Sir, I can't drive a car when the instruments are working. In fact, I removed all the connections the moment the vehicle was handed over to me by the vendor".

KEY LEARNING

Every activity needs to get internalized to bring out the designed output quality, in both services and products, meeting the voice of the customer.

4.4 MEASURE EFFECTIVELY

Remember not to neglect service and support service functions. Bring in measurements for their effectiveness.

APPRECIATION

Every organization has a principal activity and several support functions. Manufacturing companies have the production department at the core with others like materials, human resource, maintenance and quality control functions providing support services. Some of the relatively more distant functions like marketing and finance also support the production unit. The same is true with service organizations like banks, hospitals and educational institutions. For such organizations, the support functions could be the back-office, logistics, hardware maintenance and administration.

Irrespective of the type of organization, none of the principal activities can deliver results without the active support of their service functions. Unfortunately, the importance of support functions like quality and maintenance is felt only when there are problems hindering the prime function. Very often, these service functions are easy targets for passing on the buck and are remembered only when there are problems. They often receive more brickbats than bouquets. Whenever things go well without hindrances, it is the principal activity that takes the credit.

The paradox is, most organizations announce that quality is their utmost priority and that they are committed to providing the highest quality both in products and services. However, what they practice is exactly the reverse. I am aware of a paper product export organization, located in Mumbai, striving to establish its products in the USA markets, without any full-fledged quality department. More importantly, such a department was not in its plan.

Unlike the principal functions like production department or a retail store or a telecom service provider whose performances can be measured against business targets, it is somewhat difficult to measure the performance of support service functions, though not impossible. In view of their importance, their performance levels, too, should be quantified and measured. It is best to derive such measurables based on the feedback from internal and external customers. Support service functions like quality management are, necessarily, customer-focused activities and every measurable is, therefore, customer-driven.

It is not uncommon to come across a large number of measurables while managing quality. Whenever that happens, follow the priority principle that helps in identifying key measurables and then work towards achieving them.

Key areas need to be identified and performance measures need to be quantified so that the progress on each can be measured and monitored. It is a continuous process and should be addressed as such to ensure appropriateness of the measurements.

When such a comprehensive data, covering both primary and support service functions is quantified, reviewed, analyzed and improved upon, the performance management system becomes effective. A powerful tool used by successful quality managements is the annual or bi-annual service feedback reports. The reports are based on the performance appraisals from both internal and external customers. Both quantitative and qualitative attributes are considered to arrive at customer feedback indices. Once such measurements are available, they are used for targeted annual improvements.

The importance of identifying and testing the effectiveness of all the organizational processes and technologies being implemented does not take the backseat at leading companies. Yet, we often learn that, when we do not urge employees at all levels to take a hard look at what they are doing and why, they will unwittingly do **horrible** things over and over again.

Lord Kelvin, speaking to the Institute of Civil Engineers on May 3, 1883, said, "when you can measure what you are speaking about and express it in numbers, you know something about it". While we appreciate that not every fact is a numerical one and not every scientific action a predictor of numerical magnitude, it is difficult to conceive modern management without paying attention to measurement.

APPLICATION

During the 1970s when I was working with Mukand Steel, the company decided to collaborate with a consortium of Japanese steel companies for technical inputs. That was the period when Mukand was graduating from the production of mild steels meant for construction units to alloy steel products required by the engineering industry. Sanyo was a globally known special steel manufacturer, having manufacturing facilities somewhat similar to Mukand's. A collaboration agreement was drawn up, and as Chief of

Technology, I was asked to visit the plant facilities and draw up a training schedule that was mutually acceptable.

I landed at Tokyo one fine afternoon and to my amazement, came out of the airport within just 15 minutes, after completing the immigration formalities and collecting my luggage. At the beautiful and well-designed arrival lounge, I was received by Wada San, the Plant Manager of Sanyo, a short and bulky middle-aged person. The Sanyo Steel management was kind enough to send a chauffeur-driven limousine for my travel to Himeji, where the plant was located.

It was a beautiful black Toyota. The driver greeted us traditionally and politely invited us through the open door. Even though we drove at a high speed, the vehicle moved so smoothly, it hardly felt we were in a moving vehicle, except when we looked out of the window. The seats were most comfortable, covered with freshly starched white cloth and the music was soft and melodious. There were newspapers of the day, English magazines, a couple of mineral water bottles positioned at comfort levels near the back seat. Nothing seemed to be wrong with customer care in Japan.

After about 10 minutes, I found the driver looking at the dashboard and making dots on a ruled page clipped in front of him, though not losing his concentration on driving. When he did the same a couple times more, precisely at 20-minute intervals, I could not hold back my curiosity.

I asked my host what exactly the driver was noting down. After enquiring from the driver, he said that the driver was plotting temperature readings, in the form of a run chart, to check the efficiency of the air-conditioner. Only the previous day, the car had its regular servicing check-up, including the air-conditioning. He just wanted to ensure that the temperature settings were within the set limits and comfortable to his customers.

KEY LEARNING

Measurements are effective only when they impact external and internal customers.

4.5 A STITCH IN TIME

Manage improvement projects with speed. Accelerated attempts are vital to stay competitive.

APPRECIATION

In today's competitive business environment, managers cannot sit on information and data for too long without taking appropriate decisions. In my experience, decision-making is the most misunderstood term. Decisiveness is not by itself a virtue. To decide not to decide is also a decision. To fail to decide is indeed a failure. Lord Falkland's rule was, "when it is not necessary to take a decision, it is necessary not to make a decision".

Why are most managers afraid of making decisions and tend to drag on? Invariably, they are afraid that their decisions may go wrong, and believe that the best way to avoid taking any wrong decision is no–decision. They decide only when they are forced to.

The practice of making a noting, "let's discuss" is the most common escape route practiced to avoid any decision. The more the people roped in for discussion, the merrier. Any simple problem can be made complicated and insolvable if more meetings are held to discuss the same subject. Once the way to solve a problem is presented for consideration, it will invariably be accepted as the soundest solution.Once the solution ruins the project, all those who initially endorsed it will say, "I wish I had voiced my reservations at that time".

Let us look at the "7 wastes" popularly known as MUDA, developed by Toyota, to address all kinds of waste found in any manufacturing plant, or even in a service organization. They cover overproduction, time loss, unnecessary material movement, over-processing, high inventory, employee inefficiency and defects. Successfully addressing to them is the basis for just-in-time or lean philosophy. Each kind of waste calls for appropriate decision-making, that too quickly, to avoid further damage.

We all agree that defects cost money. Occurrence of defects is a challenge as well as an opportunity to improve — improve fast — rather than something to be accepted as a part of business.

During the initial period of implementation of Juran's Trilogy in India, in the early 1990s, it was not uncommon for Quality Improvement Teams to drag on with the projects even up to twelve months for completion. It was justified under the pretext that, for any structured quality improvement, a cultural change was needed within an organization. It was also justified that such a change could come about only through organizational transformation and employees' positive behavioural changes.

Over the years, it was found that such an approach was only a myth and should not be encouraged. Neither the organization nor the customer can afford the luxury of change management that takes so long for demonstration.

Currently, a three-month duration for project competition is targeted by most Improvement Teams. When projects are handled systematically, primarily through a two-stage diagnostic and a remedial journey, a short duration appears more than adequate.

When a survey was conducted on over 3,000 successful quality improvement teams, it was observed that over 80% of the projections were in fact completed within the three-month period. All that was required was focused periodic reviews with appropriate course corrections for progress.

With projects of a long duration, the teams should consider closing the projects within a three-month period even though the recorded improvements might not be in line with the targets. In such cases, the just achieved targets will be the basis for setting up new project teams with quantified new goals.

APPLICATION

It was the 23rd day of January, 1991. I was woken up suddenly at 0300 hours by an uneasy pain in my chest. Fortunately, the pain quickly subsided, allowing me to attend all my appointments of the day. When I returned late in the night, at my wife's prodding, I visited my cardiologist friend, just before his closing hours. After a few preliminary investigations, including ECG, he concluded that nothing was wrong at that moment. However, he was appreciative of our initiative to visit him, without losing any time. His passing line statement was, "Have Sorbitrate at home" – a drug which I never took in my life – "and ring me up once again, even in the middle of the night, in case the pain recurs".

I had a good night's sleep, with no indication of what was in store for me the next day. At 0600 hours I was woken up by a sudden, unusual and severe pain in the chest. The pain was quickly growing in intensity and it appeared to be a cardiac attack. Within a minute, my cardiologist was sounded, who immediately instructed my wife to place a Sobitrate tablet below my tongue and rush me to the nearest Inlak hospital, about 5 minutes' drive from my home. The doctor had already reached the hospital and kept the stretcher ready with two attendants. Within 15 minutes of the attack, I was in the ICU and was administered the life-saving drug "Streptokynacin".

Later, I was told that administering the drug within 15 minutes of the attack not only ensures cent-per cent recovery of the patient but also prevents any further damage to the heart muscles. In fact, the probability of recovery drastically comes down with an increasing time lapse between the attack and administration of the drug.

The fact that I was in ICU reached Mukand Steel, my then employer, and within half an hour or so, practically the entire plant personnel were at the hospital to see me. The authorities refused lthem permission to go near ICU, and the only exception they made was to the managing director. He too was quite concerned about my early recovery and indeed lent tremendous moral support to my family.

Everyone around was somewhat relieved at around 1000 hours when the doctors declared that I was out of danger, but needed close monitoring for the next 48 hours. There was tremendous appreciation at the way my wife handled the situation without panic and for making decisions without wasting even a single second.

Just before leaving Inlak hospital, noticing that the facilities were not so sophisticated, our managing director suggested to the cardiologist that he would prefer my shifting to Hinduja, one of the leading medical care centres in Mumbai,. about an hour's drive from Inlak. He was politely rebuked with a firm assertion that certainly, the swift action of my family had saved me, and there was no need of shifting me for the next two days. I spent my entire recuperation time at Inlak.

KEY LEARNING

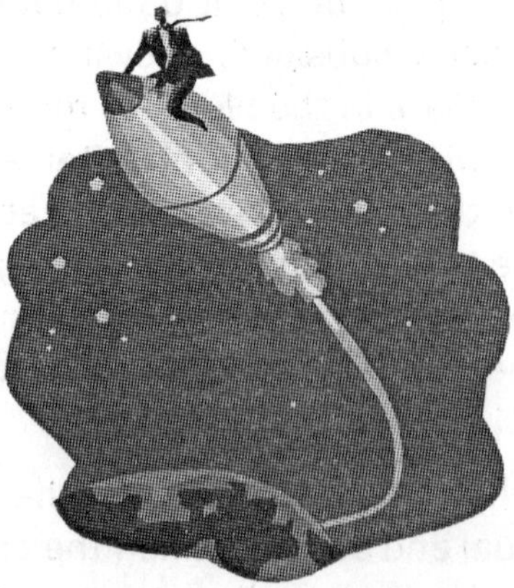

Be decisive. Move with speed.

4.6 HAVE A MEASUREMENT SYSTEM

The data and information needs to be relevant, accurate and useful. It can be ensured only through a sound measurement system.

APPRECIATION

Good decisions are based on sound information and data. Every single improvement project depends a lot on analysing available information and collected data, which in turn is based on appropriate measurements. Only relevant measurements are helpful, and what is relevant is based on the process knowledge. Once the relevance of the data is firmed up, the leading organizations' focus on data integrity would ensure that the database is reliable and dependable, that it can be subjected to a meaningful analysis.

One may often come across several important measurements that are taken from gauges which are not calibrated with desired periodicity. Even when such calibration is done, it is not uncommon to find that the measuring instruments' repeatability and reproducibility are not adequately addressed. Consequently, the data can be unreliable and unworthy for further analysis.

The measurement system analysis is an important tool in the hands of the management to critically look at the recorded data to move ahead with speed. When it is truly applied, target-setting becomes easier and proves relevant, and the milestones for progress reviews are based on sound principles. A good measurement system is a firm foundation that makes further analysis a powerful tool for managerial decisions which are based on accurate and reliable data. It is imperative to ensure that the measurements indeed generate such accurate data that it is adequate to achieve the business objective.

Measurements need to be precise and accurate. Experience has shown that 30% to 50% of measurement systems are incapable of accurately and precisely measuring the desired metric. It is essential to ensure that the differences in the data are due to actual differences in what is being measured and not due to variations in measuring methods.

Ensuring that the project teams are measuring the right material in the right way to get the right results is a must. Measurement of the final product or service characteristic is an outcome of measurement on processes. Measurement indices are the numerical measure used to guide the search for better performance. They are recognised as a means rather than an end.

Recognitions and rewards are usually based on recorded information and data. While aligning rewards with measurements, Jack Welsh talked of the universal problem: "What you measure is what you get – what you reward is what you get". The point is, therefore, are we measuring and rewarding the specific performance we want? By not aligning rewards with measurements, we often get what we are not looking for.

There is a growing awareness that it is not good to manage any activity through qualitative or vague terms. Increasingly, the improvement teams are talking in specific and measurable terms. Hence, the importance of a measurement system.

APPLICATION

Mukand Ltd., as the leading mini steel works in India has, over the years, established its capability to produce high quality carbon steel rods and bars. With the decision to broaden the company's product range, the company's metallurgists were developing austenitic stainless steel products, containing extremely low carbon levels and alloyed with 18% chromium and 8% nickel. The objective was to bring out the products which would finally have, what is known as austenitic metallurgical structure, as seen under metallurgical microscopes, at high magnification.

A key element in ensuring the non-magnetic structure is the control on what is called delta ferrite. It should not be present at all, after subjecting the necessary solution annealing treatment to the bars and rods.

These quality requirements could be certified only after the products were tested for all key parameters, including delta ferrite. The then existing metallurgical microscopes at Mukand's quality control laboratories were found inadequate to test and certify these stringent requirements.

It was felt that an accurate measurement of delta ferrite was crucial to the development. A proposal to procure and install an advanced microspore, costing around half a million rupees was sanctioned by the management, after due deliberation, and a letter of intent was issued.

Suddenly, there was an unexpected turn of events. A National Emergency was declared by the then Congress government resulting in the arrest of Mukand's managing director, who was an opposition member of parliament. The senior management was taken aback and the board had to make a decision.

As a stop gap, an aged person with finance acumen was quickly appointed as an executive director, to take charge of running the company. With very little experience in managing a metallurgical unit and with a clear mandate to safeguard the company's finances, his only objective was to save every single rupee and discourage any form of over-spending.

One of his first actions as executive director was reversing the decision of buying the advanced metallurgical microscope. He disapproved the purchase primarily since it required capital expenditure and refused to budge even after the justification noting was shown to him. He never understood the importance of measurement, and product certification based on sound measurement.

Over the next few days, he had several meetings with the senior technical team, including myself as Technical Manager, but to no avail. He decided that measurement of delta ferrite could be off-loaded to outside test laboratories and their results should be good enough for accelerating the developmental work and also for certification.

The outcome of this decision was a shame. Quite a few reports from the outside laboratories were wrong and needed close scrutiny. Further, the test results were not reaching the company on time, resulting in considerable delay in the development and product despatch. More importantly, the developmental work often took a wrong route due to inaccurate data. After a few months, the executive director left Mukand, better sense prevailed and the newly procured microscope proved to be immensely useful to stainless steel development at Mukand.

KEY LEARNING

All measurements should be reliable, accurate and relevant. Ensure robustness of the measurement system.

4.7 MAINTAIN DATA INTEGRITY

Data should always be accurate, reliable and challengeable. Data integrity is vital for working towards improvements.

APPRECIATION

Let us look at the IT industry. It breathes data. Today's IT managers are challenged with questions such as: How can we effectively manage the continually changing software environment? How can we apply a myriad of emerging tools, platforms and methodologies? How can we address and control software development issues when new technologies often compound the problem? The whole challenge boils down to the management of facts. The point is how to effectively ensure fact-based management across the organization that will succeed in this fast-changing environment.

No one doubts the importance of data. It is being widely accepted as a key resource for any successful operation. Quite often, systems are created to throw up the required data whenever asked to do so. Irrespective of the type of data entry into the system, whether off-line or on-line, the importance of data integrity can never be questioned or doubted.

Problems related to data integrity crop up primarily in large organizations, more so when their managements appear complacent. Over a period, these organizations could become so unwieldy that the internal checks, balances and counter balances may go haywire. In fact, when detected, the deficiencies will be so glaring, that they greatly surprise everyone around.

Periodic audits are expected to throw up the need for adequate measures after pinpointing deficiencies, either in the processes or systems or in their implementation. However, even the audits sometimes get "managed", thereby losing their value.

Data integrity can become questionable in two situations. Either there are genuine errors in capturing and presenting the data or there is a deliberate attempt to circumvent an uncomfortable development. The first one is not so serious since it could be easily addressed and corrected. However, the observed deficiencies should not be swept under the carpet, thereby convincing oneself that nothing wrong had happened.

Deliberate attempts to twist the data to suit one's convenience should be nipped in the bud. This tendency is far more serious, and should be squarely faced, often with the ruthlessness it deserves. Very few managers have the time, patience and desire to get into details and can be easily carried away by resorting to graphical displays through the most impressive powerpoint presentations. When such presentations are delivered by those who have excellent articulation skills, more managers can get easily fooled. By the time they wake up, probably it will be too late.

The biggest problem of data management is that it can be manipulated and interpreted in a way that suits one's logic and even its conclusions. It is only a detailed and careful analysis of the data that would bring out the errors. Experience has shown that even the most glaring errors can be hidden in deep chests.

APPLICATION

A couple of years ago, a leading organization applied for a National Award for Business Excellence. As per the globally accepted practice, a team of seasoned assessors was constituted by the award management and the application copies were sent to each team-members well in advance. The application strictly followed the guidelines, was beautifully drafted and was assessor-friendly.

After studying the contents, the assessment team was quite impressed with the number of initiatives taken by the company to make its quality conspicuous in all its operations. Excellent linkage was apparent in the application report between the management initiatives taken, deployment among all the key operations and the business results. With tremendous positive feeling, the team decided to undertake a site visit, to look for objective evidence against what had been claimed in the application report.

It was a three-day assessment, involving five assessors to cover all organizational activities. The applicant was informed of the issues which the assessor team might concentrate on, without losing sight of other related issues.

During this assessment, the leadership commitment and drive to take the company to higher levels of performance was visible. Several quality-related processes were internalised and systematized with necessary self-audits for compliance. Continuous improvement methods involved every single worker through Quality Control Circles. In fact, every single employee was involved in one or more quality improvement teams. New ideas were encouraged through suggestion schemes, and the company held a record of over 60% of suggestions successfully implemented. The skills exhibited by the employees were exemplary. Most of their presentation skills were demonstrated through sharp powerpoint slides and their key bullets were well explained.

The financial performance, as visible through a study of balance sheets, appeared quite healthy since the past five years, in spite of fierce competition for their product range, both in Indian and export markets.

At the end of the second day, there was a near unanimity among the team-members that the company was outstanding from several angles, in all assessment areas related to company's approaches, their deployment and results.

Then we made this uneasy discovery. While very exhaustive data was outlined in all key operational areas, along with periodic reviews, there were a few mismatches. Evidently, a huge bank of data related to shift-wise and day-wise operations was getting generated. The data was then consolidated as weekly and monthly reports for appropriate reviews. Special attention was paid to bring out colourful graphs and charts for such reviews. The data and information was then escalated to quarterly reviews by the senior management.

The assessment team made a critical study on the review process adopted by the company at various levels.

The first observation was that the reviews were primarily aimed at stock taking. Since the organization was "apparently" performing very well with sound financials, a certain degree of casualness crept into its approach.

The second, and in fact the most damaging one, was related to glaring inconsistencies in the data presented at various fora. This had come to light when the assessment team wondered why the organization was showing undue interest in converting most of the simple straightforward data into ratios. Several inconsistencies were thrown up when the team-members took the trouble of recalculating the ratios. Obviously, the data was manipulated for convenience.

Consequently, the assessment team concluded that there was no integrity in data collection, analysis and presentation, and the applicant was wittingly or unwittingly moving away from operational excellence.

KEY LEARNING

Data integrity is ensured only by demonstrating honesty at all levels. Senior management should take complete ownership to make it happen.

5 Chapter

PAY ATTENTION TO HUMAN ELEMENT

Behind every successful initiative and its management is the human face providing a powerful support system.

CONTENTS

5.1 BE PERSISTENT

Be persistent in your efforts. It is easier to fail in an improvement effort. The challenge lies in making it successful.

APPRECIATION

Let us appreciate that in this open business society, most executives are proving to be smarter, cannot be easily carried away and are more thorough in dealing with the real world. There is less room to wriggle out of poorly conceived and ill-planned situations. One cannot handle a smart executive with inadequate preparation.

On the other hand, most stakeholders, including employees, customers and suppliers are getting increasingly less tolerant. The fallacy is while they are not ego-free, they expect professional and ego-free leadership, with a human touch from others. Each executive is a different type of person, who has great opportunity to shape the most dynamic time in the history of the world, and we have no other option than to deal with him.

Managerial arrogance is the tragedy of the current society. The top management, whether they were born for the job or rose up from lower ranks through merit and hard work, is exhibiting increasing levels of arrogance. This needs to be squarely faced. As Lord Acton said, "Power corrupts, and absolute power corrupts absolutely". It is not always possible to handle life and work on our own. We must learn to manage in all types of situations and emerge successful.

New technologies and new management tools are posing further challenges, though they do not necessarily lead to new levels of comprehension, learning and competence by themselves. However, if we do not keep up with the technology of learning, we will certainly fall further behind.

Leadership never manages in isolation. As Crosby said, for being a leader, treat the whole as one, build a culture of consideration, make everything understood and complete but not finished. Leadership functions, therefore, need a lot of perseverance to succeed. Quite often, most functions are so busy in handling the routine, they hardly find time to provide necessary support to other functions and prefer operating in silos.

A common mistake most organizations make is creating separate functions, believing them to be standalones. Creation of a quality control department for solving all quality problems is a classic blunder. It only provides an escape route through the belief that every quality failure can be directly attributable to this department, while several others have a role to play to ensure quality in both products and services. Quality management is not an isolated activity, nor can it be managed as a standalone function. Since it interfaces with several functions and activities, quality needs to be managed in a structured manner.

Whenever new initiatives are taken up by an organization, unless there is a high level of commitment and involvement, particularly at the top management level, one may end up with several explanations on why they have failed. It is easy to figure out what went wrong and blame everyone around for the failure.

The challenge lies in making every management initiative successful. This calls for clearly set goals, periodic reviews with appropriate course corrections, and both vertical and horizontal involvement across the organization. It is amazing how much a person, with an unshaken commitment, can accomplish. An essential requisite is to have patience and perseverance at all levels to make every initiative a success.

To quote Dale Carnegie, "most of the important things in this world have been accomplished by people who have kept on trying when there seemed to be no hope at all".

APPLICATION

There is this famous story of King Robert the Bruce, the heroic King of the Scots, who secured Scotland's independence from England.

Robert was born on 11 July, 1274 into an aristocratic Scottish family and supported William Wallace's uprising against the English. After Wallace was defeated, Bruce became a guardian of Scotland. The following year, Bruce was deposed by the English King Edward's army and forced to flee. His wife and daughters were imprisoned and three of his brothers executed. Robert spent the winter on the island off the coast of Antrim (Northern Ireland).

Returning to Scotland, Robert waged a highly successful guerrilla war against the English. At the Battle of Bannockburn in June 1314, he defeated a much larger English army under Edward II, confirming the reestablishment of an independent Scottish monarchy.

He renewed the Franco-Scottish alliance by which the Scots were obliged to make war on England should hostilities break out between England and France. In 1327, the

English deposed Edward II in favour of his son and peace was made with Scotland. This included a total renunciation of all English claims to superiority over Scotland.

Robert was both brave and wise, because the times in which he lived were wild and dangerous. He fought battle after battle with England. He had led his brave little army six times against his foes. His men had been beaten six times, until finally, they were driven to flight. At last the army of Scotland was entirely scattered, and the King was forced to hide in the woods and in lonely places among the mountains.

One rainy day, Robert the Bruce lay in a cave, listening to the rainfall outside the cave entrance. He was tired and felt sick at heart, ready to give up all hope. It seemed to him that there was no use for him to try to do anything more.

As he lay thinking, he noticed a spider over his head, getting ready to weave her thread from one edge of the cave wall to another. Six times she threw her thread but it fell short. "Poor thing!" said Robert. "You, too, know what it's like to fail six times in a row."

But the spider did not lose hope. Carefully, she made ready to try a seventh time. Robert almost forgot his own troubles as he watched, fascinated. She swung herself out upon the slender line. Would she fail again? No! The thread was carried safely to the cave wall, and fastened there. "Yes!" cried Bruce, "I, too, will try a seventh time!" He did it.

Robert died on 7 June, 1329.

KEY LEARNING

Several roadblocks crop up while implementing new initiatives.
Face them squarely with perseverance.

5.2 LISTEN TO LEAD

Two important attributes contributing towards outstanding performance are: listen and lead.

APPRECIATION

Montgomery, the British Field Marshal, once described leadership as the capacity and will to rally men and women to a common purpose and as the character that inspires confidence. How do we, as leaders, inspire confidence in others? It is possible only through attentively listening to and involving others. As the leadership proverb goes, "If you think you are leading and no one is following you, then you're only taking a walk".

A good leader is certainly a good listener, though all listeners are not good leaders. He encourages everyone around, without exception, to say what he should know rather than what he likes to hear. Personal meetings with such leaders leave pleasant memories and business meetings are interactive, since everyone is encouraged to talk and listen. It is known that 60 per cent of all managerial problems are the result of faulty communication, and an overwhelming majority of these problems comes from poor listening.

Leaders love to listen to their customers, employees, suppliers, market forces, competition and the like, and get updated continuously. The busiest leaders always have time to meet at leisure and are almost always available for interactions. When it comes to customers, several leading companies follow the disciplined practice of escalating customer feedback, including complaints, first to their CEOs. The very fact that the top man is listening directly from his customers amply demonstrates seriousness and ensures early resolution.

I am aware of several outstanding technology leaders, both in India and abroad, who love to network with their own peer groups. They meet at regular intervals at rotating locations, attentively listen to each other and exchange notes on their latest hands-on experiences, with no fixed agenda. Some of these interactive meetings are found so valuable the members eagerly look forward to participating in these meetings.

At operating levels, even in an active team deliberation, out of ten participants, only one or two are good listeners. Many participants only hear and pick up just the decibels. To make sense they need to listen. They are not attentive, show little patience and enjoy cross talk that results in confusion and non-focused deliberation. The outcome is, invariably, unproductive.

Listening is a skill. Most managers develop this skill by practice. A good listening skill makes others comfortable to communicate. They feel satisfied that their view points were being heard with the attention they deserve.

During the problem solving process, aiming at continuous improvements, each team decides on its course of action based on the inputs from team-members, both verbal and written, with appropriate quantification. At the meetings, the team leaders listen carefully to assure every member of the team that his or her views, when put across properly, do get the attention of all. Participation, then, is no compulsion but is an enjoyment.

In this age of Information Technology, when unlimited data and information is available to us at a finger-click through media like the internet, it is not the quantum of data that is important, but the relevance of the data. If the data presented by any stakeholder is not sharply focussed or its relevance questioned, it is unlikely to get much attention. Leaders with a sharp eye for detail can easily see through it and politely avoid dragging on such meetings.

APPLICATION

When desktop computers made their entry into offices and began changing work culture, including the way correspondence is handled and calculations made, the top management of a leading Indian business group was in a fix.

Overruling concerns from his senior colleagues, the managing director took a snap decision to change his company into a paperless one, in one go. He was sold on the idea of being one the earliest companies to do so, and sought everyone's cooperation to make this happen. "The decision of computerisation isn't open for discussion", he said, "but the concern should be how fast this could be implemented".

The younger managers were thrilled with their high tech toys. They were keen on quickly becoming proficient with their personal computers, and decided to invest their time and effort to learn and use them to the maximum. However, the older managers, who were a majority, tried their hand at the computers, but with little success.

The seniors knew that electronic communication had come to their organization to stay in. They knew they might be sidetracked if they did not soon become computer-savvy. There was also an element of fear that the senior management would, without much delay, take alternate steps to fill in the technology usage gap, and in extreme cases, recruit computer-savvy fresh hands.

The case of Prasad, an in-charge of production planning, was a typical one. A sincere, hardworking executive, he was always afraid of adopting anything new, and was among those who panicked with this development. Despite his best efforts, he picked up very little from the crash course conducted by the suppliers of the battery of computers. Fear took a toll on his health and affected even his normal work.

But the managing director did not make this an issue. He quickly reviewed and analysed the situation. He heard each one patiently and assured everyone that they would be given adequate opportunity to learn and that he had the patience to wait. Besides, he said that he had nothing to fear about Prasad.

The top management felt that the training by the suppliers was somewhat theoretical and not so user-friendly to slow learners. The seniors were trained at a computer institute through hands-on methods, including classroom lectures and practicals conducted by young but experienced teachers. The company paid for this education. The lectures were on eight Saturdays and the managers got compensatory off for attending the training sessions on holidays. The company also covered the costs for local commuting, lunch, tea and snacks.

The results were excellent. The senior managers soon became PC savvy and began working in unison with the youngsters and also among themselves. The company soon demonstrated positive improvements with desired performance.

KEY LEARNING

Listen to appreciate and act. Ensure that analysis does not lead to paralysis.

5.3 PRACTICE THE PREACH

Practice what you preach. People follow the leaders who are role models.

APPRECIATION

It is easy to give a sermon, but difficult to practice. My mother-in-law who is now eighty-five gets up daily at 0530 hours to sit before her favourite TV programmes where enlightened souls give lectures on spiritual values, surrender to the superior and, virtues like detachment in attachment and attachment in detachment. When we look at their dyed jet black hair, expensive clothing and exquisite precious stone studded rings on all their fingers, their discourses could be uncomfortable to many.

We have medical practitioners who do not tire of explaining to all around the harmful effects of smoking, while continuing to be chain smokers. An obese orthopaedic surgeon friend of mine continued to be a fast-food freak and had cardiac arrest at the young age of forty-five.

Among the many managerial interfunctional activities, good coaching stands out, since it is a product of personal qualities and demonstrated interpersonal skills. Coaching succeeds under a proper climate and a two-way participation with subordinates is a must for effective coaching. A hostile climate is obviously not conducive to effective coaching.

Situations demonstrating positive vibrations benefit more from coaching than others. A better coach needs to pay attention to the psychological climate in which coaching takes place. The climate is characterized by several intangible but important features such as mutual trust, motivation to learn and improve, and accountability for results.

Coaching is a manager's important function, demanding his most valuable and limited resource, namely time. All managers appear pressed for time since they are engaged mostly in routine activities, and thus, though competent, under-invest in coaching.

Some managers have the extraordinary capability to talk endlessly on any topic of discussion. They dictate and direct too much and listen too little. They want us to believe they know all. Their contribution may appear valid and significant at that moment, may make sense and appear impressive, but do not carry conviction. Such persons cannot be good coaches.

If coaching inputs create applicability problems, difficulties are bound to crop up when these inputs are put to practice. Talking to employees won't do much good if they are not motivated and encouraged to listen.

The applicability component is important not only for processes but also in systems. While detailing the best system, it is helpful if the system is supported by easy applicability and successful application. Such applications get firmly registered in the minds of the employees. They may be further supplemented with enhanced learning through visible successes.

Leaders have to be good role models. They cannot afford to lose control of their emotions. They should not preach anything to subordinates and direct them to do something he or she would resist, without emotional preparation. The ultimate weapon in coaching is the leader's own on-the-spot behaviour.

Any subordinate can understand goals and why they are important, but he or she must also be motivated to pursue the goals. You can coach this same person to close individual and organizational performance gaps, but the employee won't take that coaching to heart if he or she is uninterested or unmotivated.

As a leader, we are being watched by all our colleagues and peers. They observe how we behave, perform, delegate, communicate, motivate and coach towards continual learning and improvement. Many of them may be patterning their own behaviour on ours. Hence, it is imperative for the leaders to set high personal standards of behaviour and performance that they would want their followers to adopt.

APPLICATION

Gandhi is the best symbol of "practicing the preach". Whatever your position in an organizational setup, whether you are a profit centre head or an ordinary staff member, Gandhi's relevance is expressed in these lines from *Bhagavad Gita*:

Work is holy.

When the heart of the worker

Is fixed on the highest,

Action rightly performed brings freedom.

In other words, it is not what you do but the spirit in which you commit to work that is important. For Gandhi, the spinning wheel was a symbol of the dignity of work, no matter how simple it looks.

As Gandhi legatee Dr. Martin Luther King later explained, "No work is insignificant. All labour that uplifts humanity has dignity and importance, and should be undertaken with painstaking excellence. If a man is called to be a street-sweeper, he should sweep the streets even as Michelangelo painted, or Beethoven composed music, or Shakespeare wrote poetry. He should sweep the streets so well that all the hosts of heaven and earth will pause to say: 'Here lived a great street-sweeper who did his job well'".

Marcia Wieder, the bestselling author of *Making Your Dreams Come True*, commented on Gandhi as an inspiration in his own work.

"As a professional speaker and motivator, I'm often asked where I get my motivation. Well, there is a statue of Gandhi near my home in San Francisco. For years I have visited this place. It has become a sacred spot for me. I approach this master with reverence. I make eye contact with him as I stand in light of sight. I open my heart, and a question always bubbles up from the depth of my soul. The answers that I receive from him are priceless.

He tells me, 'Feel my peace, feel my soul, feel yourself as me, know us as one. Begin here. Our beating heart is the pulse of the universe. It is the one vibration. Slow down and be quiet to know this pulse. Beyond thinking, beyond feeling, come to know. Then may you speak it, then may you share it. Go deeper, deeper, deeper'.

"Gandhi provides me with much needed messages I long to hear. Always delivered with piercing clarity and sweet simplicity. Sometimes, when I feel tired, afraid or confused, invoking his presence reminds me that I have a calling, a unique purpose, a reason why I am here. My destiny is to lead so I may follow, to teach so I may learn, to communicate so I may hear. Gandhi is more than a role model, he is a living presence who reminds us that gentleness can move mountains and that a still place of oneness lives in all of our hearts".

Mahatma Gandhi continues to be an inspiration to many.

KEY LEARNING

It is easier to preach than to be a role model.

Only performers carry conviction.

5.4 MIND YOUR ATTITUDE

Quality is a product of ability and attitude.

APPRECIATION

A number of descriptions exist for "quality" in literature. To me, quality of any performance is a result of judicious application of abilities and attitudes.

For high quality performance, ability and attitude should be conspicuous in abundance, in every corner of the application arena. Most on-the-job training modules address enhancement of skills, with little or no attention to attitudinal issues. While improved skills help to do a job better they do not, by themselves, make a person committed to do better.

Phil Clements describes that a positive person is non-judgemental, in control of self and situations, creative in thinking and planning, able to cope with and manage change, optimistic, and able to communicate effectively all the attributes above. Further, a truly positive person can recognise the negatives and also has the skills necessary to handle them.

During our daily life, we experience several thoughts converting them into actions such as planning, conversing, sharing and implementing. In all these actions, attitudes are conspicuous, both positive and negative. If any one believes that he is born either positive or negative, that he is destined to be like that by birth, and that he has to live with it, he is sadly mistaken. On the other hand, positive attitudes can be cultivated believing that no one is born positive, and can learn and practice to be positive.

Unless employees are passionately committed to perform, no management initiative, however great, will deliver results. Empowering employees, without adequate preparation is a sure invitation to chaos. It is essential that organizations distinguish between

"Training for Quality" and "Training for Skills", and recognize that both need increasing focus. It is primarily the senior management that can drive and facilitate operational excellence through attitudinal deployment.

Among the key attributes addressed through this management approach are:

- Competence creation
- Focused commitment
- Perseverance
- Managing expertise
- Shared values

Employee behaviour is a reflection of his or her attitude towards an organization and its stakeholders. Unless critical aspects of this behaviour, affecting the stated values, are detailed and precisely defined, the odds are it cannot be changed.

By measuring employee behaviour — be it at the individual, team and organizational level — it becomes tangible and specific. Measurements allow abstract to become concrete and obscure the specific. Now that quality management through quantification is well established, even the so-called abstract issues like attitude are being successfully addressed through structured improvement methodologies.

While measuring attitudes, it is not enough to simply provide a measure of the current state; but should provide measurable inputs for both diagnostics and remedials so as to overcome deficiencies and move forward.

APPLICATION

Among my first experiences as Manager – Quality Control was to address a severe quality complaint on drawability of high carbon steel wire rods. A leading wire drawing unit, located in Kolkata, found it difficult to draw them into wires and twist them to the required size since the high carbon wire rods supplied by the steel plant did not have the desired torsional ductility.

My scientific investigation on this customer complaint clearly established that the rods, supplied to the customer were not of consistent quality. The investigation showed that there were several lapses on the part of the plant, as shown by the production reports of both steel making and casting, and product quality studies. My report clearly highlighted several process deficiencies and concluded that poor quality of wire rods was in fact the primary cause for the drawability and torsional ductility difficulties at the customer's end.

The report further indicated that the plant had the necessary technical capability and adequate product and process standards to ensure the quality levels required by the wire drawing unit, and the lapses were attributable to a lack of committed implementation of the standards.

The report was discussed internally at various levels of the organization. It so happened that, as quality manager, I was then reporting to the General Manager-Marketing who was concurrently holding the post of General Manager-Works, due to the resignation of the latter.

My boss questioned the report and asked for a reinvestigation which only confirmed the earlier findings. However, he maintained that there was nothing wrong with the wire rods and the problem was at the customer's end, during the drawing process. He even went to the extent of suggesting that the investigative report should be modified to show that the drawability problems were essentially due to deficiencies at the drawing stage.

I refused to change the contents of the report. My stand was that every single technical report should be based on facts and should carry a honest interpretation, without any bias. Any interference in the working of quality assurance function would be unethical and highly detrimental to the integrity of the organization. During all this turmoil, in spite of repeated follow-ups, the customer was kept in dark.

Soon, the matter went directly from the customer to the managing director who was immediately fed with a copy of the technical report prepared by an external agency engaged by my boss to investigate the problem, without my knowledge. The report's findings were naturally tutored to be in line with the stand taken by my boss.

The managing director then queried why I, the quality chief of the plant, was kept out of the loop. He asked for details of the internal investigation findings and obtained specific clarifications. Once all the relevant details were provided, it took barely two hours for him to accept my report in toto. He immediately passed an order accepting the complaint without any hesitation and taking the necessary action to settle this complaint.

Within a month, the General Manager-Marketing was compelled to put in his papers.

KEY LEARNING

Focus on all key attributes. Paying attention to only one attribute does not provide the adequate help in performance dynamics.

5.5 CRITICIZE TO COMPLEMENT

Criticize only if you must.
Ensure that every critical comment is supplemented with suggestions for possible improvement.

APPRECIATION

We often come across people who believe they are born to criticize. Every single action is criticisable, since one can always think of an action better than the current one. Healthy criticism is not only beneficial but also essential for successful management. It throws up several issues, which are otherwise likely to be missed out on any managerial journey.

Criticisms are primarily of three types. Negating statements for the sake of criticizing are of the first type. Such statements do more harm than good and should be totally discouraged. The second type is where criticisms are usually supported with some reasoning, even though it may not necessarily find acceptance. The third type of criticism, apart from providing the reasoning also helps in an objective assessment of a situation, throws up several possible solutions and helps correct the situation.

Habitual critics love to criticize for the heck of it and enjoy being critical. They have very little to offer beyond being just a critic. They love to find faults, dig into loopholes and always have ready comments like, "It won't work that way". A classic example is, "It works in Japan, but won't work in India".

Such critics have a tendency to be anecdotal to justify their criticism. They want us to believe: "It didn't work a few years back and hence it won't work now". Most of them are good to audit and find faults. Often, they are loners and fail to be team-members, nor can they be good mentors. Since they rarely look into the positives of others, though many of them are so self-centric, they believe themselves to be extraordinarily brilliant and several notches above others. Habitual critics are professionally weak and have a tendency to be operationally weak too. Their criticism is highly personality-oriented and is not issue-based.

Reasoning critics are those who have a job knowledge and hence the capacity to justify their criticism. Since they are in the know of the subject, they are taken relatively more seriously, in comparison to the habitual critics. Their inputs, though may not be always pleasant and useful, are likely to receive due attention mainly due to their knowledge levels.

Genuine critics are highly respected since they do criticise only after due deliberation. They think twice before venturing to criticise. They criticize only when it is a must and do so with considerable dignity, since they love not to hurt. They work hard to ensure that their inputs add value. They are always well-prepared and love to be well respected since they are not insincere and cynic.

It is a challenge to be, and considered to be, a genuine critic. Apart from their positive inputs, critics can be considered genuine when they are pleasant to converse with. People can be found to be genuine by the words they love to use, the tone of voice they adopt, the content of what they say and also the non-verbal behaviour they use.

Lastly, genuine criticisms also have time and situation relevance, and cannot be indefinitely postponed. The challenge of the management is not only to seek genuine criticism but also seek them in time and get suggestions that will help create the right type of atmosphere towards improved processes, systems, products and service.

APPLICATION

During the early 1980s, both the manufacturing and the service units across the globe felt the need to evolve international standards for quality systems, which were later popularised as the ISO 9000 family of standards. The primary objective was to ensure consistency in the quality levels of current performance, across all functions of any organization. These standards, first published in the year 1989, were later revised in the years 1994 and 2000, till the date of writing this book.

The primary requirement for every company seeking ISO certification is that it should document all its key processes in the form of an apex manual with supporting procedures and work instructions, in line with the practices followed, and create appropriate records that would provide objective evidence of their compliance. The underlining benefit, due to this certification, is system creation that would insulate an organization from process inconsistencies.

By the early 1990s, due to the opening up of Indian economy, an increasingly large number of organizations started critically looking into ISO 9000 benefits and adopting the standards.

Since these standards were aimed at creating quality consistency, the maiden issue of 1989 attracted several critical comments from both quality professionals and operating managers. A common restraint was that even if an organization produces junk, as long as it consistently produces the same, it could be called an ISO certified organization.

This criticism found acceptance by many companies that were averse to documentation and its subsequent compliance, as demonstrated during audits, both internal and external. One of the large Indian business groups, controlling over thirty diversified interests, did not find the need to adopt this standard, even after ten years of its publication. When I started my association with the group in 1997, as chief of corporate quality, one of the early proposals to the board was that all the units should work towards ISO 9000.

In the very first meeting, this proposal was turned down primarily through the intervention of a senior board member, who felt that such a standard would not add any value to the group companies. His arguments were driven by his conviction, based purely on the negative experiences, as detailed in the literature. Later, I found that he had no prior discussion or analysis with his colleagues, before expressing his views on this vital subject.

During the subsequent board meeting, when this proposal came up for reconsideration, his comments were caustic and somewhat negative. He just went on cutting off the proposal without appreciating the basis on which this standard was created. He continued to be adamant and maintained that the standard was inadequate and could be more harmful than helpful.

When asked for the specifics of his reasoning, he was non-convincing. He was not aware of how international standards get evolved, approved for publication, and get implemented. While agreeing that process consistency was very important and should be addressed by every management, he had little to offer as an alternate proposal to address this deficiency.

Finally, the board took note of the likely benefits by adopting the standard while appreciating that no standard is static and gets revised periodically, to continuously incorporate improvements, based primarily on the inputs during its implementation. Once the board decided to encourage all its group companies to be ISO certified, within the next couple of years, every single unit of the group was ISO certified.

KEY LEARNING

Genuine criticism is always welcome and is encouraged.

Often critical observations from third parties can bring about unexpected benefits.

5.6 VALUE KNOWLEDGE BASE

Ensure that every single activity is knowledge-based. Even the competency to select and analyze the right information is knowledge.

APPRECIATION

All processes, whether manufacturing or non-manufacturing, can be broken up into several process steps and attention to highest performance at each of these steps is crucial. Even an apparently minor deficiency could cause havoc, and any corrective step will then be only reactive.

Experience has shown that performance through focused application of knowledge is far superior to others and is quickly recognizable. Problems often need a judicious combination of short-term and long-term solutions. Leading organizations attempt to solve these problems with permanent solutions so that they are irreversible. The problems addressed are ensured to be real and their influence on retarding the organizational growth undisputed. Every precaution is taken to ensure that problems that are imaginary, irrelevant and instantaneous are not addressed.

The tendency to quickly diagnose every problem and always arrive at a quick-fix solution, using available information, should be discouraged. Several run-of-the-mill managements encourage only such talents and recognize only such individuals. "Solve the problem quickly" is the instruction and "I have solved it" is the quick response. This apparent response is even employed for chronic problems. The problem will then recur with vengeance. However, information and intuition are often the winners.

The IT industry is quick to recognise the contribution of knowledge workers and address their needs for its own survival. This industry is aware that the knowledge workers are the backbone of all its operations and attempts to handle each one with the utmost attention. The same is true of pharmaceutical units with high research and development content. However, several manufacturing setups, with a high level frontline labour force, continue to be indifferent to the contributions that can be made by the knowledge-base. This happens primarily because they fail to manage the knowledge workers.

During my tenure with both the manufacturing companies and service units, and also through my association with many professional and social bodies, I have come across several knowledgeable persons, some humble and yet others who are somewhat difficult to deal with. A critical analysis of their characteristics revealed that they can be broadly grouped under five categories:

Sagacious: those who are wise, exceptionally intelligent, shrewd and yet easy to deal with;

Scintillating: those who sparkle through outstanding contributions and take pride in everything they succeed;

Sensitive: those who are sharp, get easily carried away with both successes and failures, and can't withstand even minor criticism;

Secretive: those who tend to be aloof, not trusting anyone around and fearful;

Selfish: those believing only in themselves.

Any management has to deal with such a diverse group of employees. It is indeed a challenge which can be squarely addressed only when each manager knows his job, knows that he knows his job, and makes it known to everyone around that he knows his job.

APPLICATION

How are quality directors appointed at senior levels? This story is hilarious.

A leading business group in India once found itself in a tricky situation. A smart guy was appointed as a general manager to look after the administrative and other support functions in one of its group companies. After a few months in the office, he thought that he deserved a promotion as a vice-president. He told the management in so many words and conveyed that he might have to seek other avenues, if the organization felt that he could not be promoted.

The top management was in a fix. The management was keen to retain him since he was smart and was useful as an allrounder. More importantly, his proximity to the top management was rather high and that naturally mattered.

Consequently, the senior management was keen to create a new position of vice-president. Since elevating him to this position required that he be given an additional responsibility, the TQM function was tagged on though he had no prior experience of quality management. Since he had not attended any quality management programmes earlier, nor did he get trained in any of the quality management processes globally practiced, he was soon uncomfortable in this new position.

Naturally, the new quality boss did not attend any project reviews nor did he guide any project team. Among the first things he did was insulate project teams from any direct access or contact with the top management. Instead, he started collating the project progress from all the teams and sending consolidated weekly reports to the top management himself.

He tried to take all credit for himself and make everyone believe that ever since he took charge, there had been tremendous progress in quality management. Soon, he began getting information on the progress in other group companies and tried to project that his contribution was the highest among the group companies.

This vice-president would often stay only at the corporate office, hardly visiting the locations where TQM was being implemented. Being position-conscious, he enjoyed administering the quality by sending his juniors for the review meetings just to collect hard and soft copies of their power point presentations.

Very soon the management realised that his only contribution was to be present at the inaugurals of quality meetings and at prize distributions. His credibility was the lowest when the management sought an assessment from the quality teams about his usefulness to the quality movement. Very soon, the group had to disengage his services.

Such quality drivers are only just 'functional' managers.

KEY LEARNING

Knowledge-based management can be easily distinguished from one that is information-based.

5.7 FACILITATE AND BE FACILITATED

Facilitate important improvements across the organization on a continuous basis. Avoid policing.

APPRECIATION

All leading organizations improve continuously. Internal improvements, both continuous and breakthrough, are so well institutionalised, they are often conspicuous as an integral part of organizational culture. However, not always can such improvements take place without appropriate intervention through external sources. That is when facilitation helps. Facilitation is an important input in making improvements happen and most companies do not hesitate to provide this add-on competence. Facilitation is both an art and a science.

Project teams do need facilitation as they progress along the problem-solving journey. The teams may get stuck along the journey, or sometimes go tangential, when the need for additional inputs is felt. The teams then require timely help to remove roadblocks and achieve desired results.

Success in any activity is facilitated or hindered by the existence or absence of support resources. No matter how competent and motivated an employee is, his or her performance is bound to suffer if there is no supportive work environment. Facilitation helps create such an environment.

While forming problem-solving teams, managements look for people with operational and technical expertise, problem-solving skills and an ability to prioritise problems, generate solutions, evaluate them, and make competent choices.Teams also need people competent to resolve conflicts and other interpersonal aberrations. While conflict by itself is not bad, since it stimulates discussion, promotes critical assessment of problems and options, and leads to better team decisions, it is often essential to moderate to ensure that it is resolved in time, well before matters get out of hand. No team can achieve full performance without addressing these aspects, where again facilitation adds value.

Team effectiveness gets a beating whenever teams create negative synergy. This could happen when the performance of some of the team-members is well below expectation or when individual team-members commit less effort when working collectively than when working individually. Also, while in teams, individuals tend to show-off their importance and resist change, and this could have a negating effect. Facilitation can be very effective under such circumstances, thereby reducing resistance and increasing participation.

Facilitators should be acceptable to the team-members. Superiors should resist the temptation of imposition. The facilitators' knowledge level should be higher than the team-members and they should have the capacity to articulate with conviction and commitment.

Facilitators are always participative with positive communication skills and provide their viewpoint in simple and clear terms, easily understood by everyone around. They have a clear and free-flowing thought process, which would not cause, or enhance the already existing, confusion among the team-members.

Facilitators are good listeners. They are patient and encourage every team-member to air his or her views without any fear or favour. They do not interject while others speak out but only try to supplement another's thoughts. Only when discussions go tangential, or not focused, or not in line with the objectives do facilitators step-in, give clear direction, and bring the discussions back into focus. They appreciate that mere teaching and leaving people to fend for themselves will not help to produce results. Facilitators love to be enablers, helping people to put into practice what they have learnt by constant guidance, assistance and support.

A facilitator ensures he is never seen as biased towards a section of the team, even if that section is friendlier to him than the other. Nor do facilitators get influenced by the hierarchical positions or seniority or educational background of the team-members. Facilitators aim only at the team's progress and continuously provide direction towards its objectives.

While leading organizations internalise the facilitation competence for their improvement projects, they are also open to engaging the help of external resource persons, whenever and wherever required.

APPLICATION

About a decade ago, Kobe Engineering, a subsidiary of Kobe Steel Japan, decided to outsource their requirements of track shoes for its earthmoving division. After skirting around for a week, through a team of four specialist managers, KE zeroed in on a small steel foundry in Hyderabad, the capital of Andhra Pradesh, a southern state in India.

The entire Indian foundry fraternity was aghast at this development. But the KE team had looked at the only positive aspect in this, and that was the management's willingness to change and learn to continuously improve. The KE told them that they should be prepared for a paradigm shift in every single management practice. The CEO of the foundry and his entire team committed themselves to revise their activities. KE entered into a contract with the foundry to underwrite all its capacities to KE's requirement.

As the first step, KE trained every single employee. They evolved a training calendar for the following twelve months, and implemented it meticulously. Initially, there were no measurements whatsoever and no standards to follow. Everything had to be evolved, developed and complied with. The standards set by KE were so stringent, initially it was hard for the foundry to follow and everyone thought it would be impossible to ensure cent per cent compliance.

Within a year of KE's association, there was visible transformation at the foundry. Every employee was participating in the quality process and ensuring the meeting of set targets. More importantly, they began getting accustomed to stringent quality levels and proactively setting up stretch targets.

During the early months, most attention was paid to creating discipline in conforming to the laid-down standards. This was followed by developing competency to focus on data creation and analysis. Application of quality improvement tools was made mandatory in all areas for improvement. While teaching these tools was relatively easy, developing capability to apply them in each operation of the company was quite a challenge, but was quickly overcome.

Facilitation accelerated the organizational transformation. Within a few months, the company recorded a remarkable improvement. From a 3 per cent defect level, most key operations touched around 0.003 per cent, a 1,000 times improvement.

The entire plant was converted into a visible factory with prominent displays all around: "Facilitate and get facilitated".

KEY LEARNING

Facilitation is a powerful tool.

Apply it at every process step.

5.8 INSPIRE AND IGNITE

Recognize creativity and reward it in time. Make it a habit.

APPRECIATION

As Drucker says, "the management's job is to make human strength productive". Unfortunately, most Indian managements believe that focussing on the economic interest of their employees is adequate. Other interests like intellect and their promotion, which also affect the performance, are hardly encouraged.

The potential for human imagination is unlimited. It only needs kindling. While continuous learning, improvements and enhanced performances are well understood by most companies, they do not look beyond these issues, but rest satisfied after they are practiced. They are barely aware that most employees are underutilised, and their huge potential is yet to be tapped.

Most employees are competent to create their own future. A man's family background, his training, his attitudes and aptitudes do help enhancing this competence. Since actions are conceived by the mind and carried out by the hands, the mind must be free to direct the action based on reason and not emotion or passion. Everyone loves to be inspired and take pride when their minds are ignited. Managements have a responsibility to make employees think and add power to their thoughts, since thoughts are the first steps of creativity.

Most people's thoughts are so self-contained, they do not really amount to much outside their own mind and body. It is said that only about 10 per cent of the population uses both sides of the brain, the left logical hemisphere and the right creative one, at the same time. This could be enhanced through boundary-less thoughts and actions with equal emphasis on the dualism of the universe.

It is important to promote the realisation that failure is foundation to success, and give and take is a part of nature. In this dual aspect of nature, every thought we produce brings in corresponding ripples and very action that we carry out brings in corresponding reaction. Thus, every action follows reaction, every inspiration follows expiration, and every part brings out its counterpart.

While understanding and memory are too complex to theorize, with constant practice they could be improved. As a result of the work done by several psychologists, different types of memory such as sensory memory, short-term memory and long-term memory have been evolved in the past four decades. Each one can be managed, and has a role to play in managing the events.

Many achievers have found inspiration for their works in dreams, and enjoyed their freedom. It was said that, Albert Einstein, while lying on a hill top on a summer day, imagined taking a ride through the universe on one of the sunbeams. His imagination was so fertile that he realised the inadequacy of his physics knowledge, pursued the path shown by his imagination and invented new mathematics that led him to the discovery of the theory of relativity.

As intelligence grows, man is in a position to integrate the impact of today's actions and aspirations with the past and also with the future. He recognises that, for him, yesterday is history, today is vision and tomorrow is challenge. As Krishnamurthy said, "Intelligence is amalgamation of the past with the present".

How do managements inspire their employees? Just encourage and enthuse, provide them a huge canvas, and recognise their contributions on time. Anything that gets recognised and rewarded gets repeated. Timely recognitions and rewards for any good performance is an important component of enlightened management.

It is also necessary to ensure non-partisan recognition conspicuous throughout the organisation. Recognition, even if a simple pat on the back, enthuses people to be proud of their achievements and the outcome could be beyond imagination and logic. That helps in creating an outstanding employee-pool. By ensuring recognition for the efforts put in, processes employed and the deliverables, leading organizations are constantly benefited through innovative ideas of relevance.

APPLICATION

This is the story of 'walkman', the tape player we all walked around with before i-pods hit the stands.

Sony wanted to come out with a new product of its own choice, and make it to sell, rather than develop one after finding out what customers wanted.

One day Ibuka, the founder of Sony, expressed his idea to Morita, Chief of Operations, "I would like to listen to music, but do not want to disturb others while I do so. I cannot sit near a stereo all day. The only solution is, I take the music with me. But it is too heavy. I would like to put forward the idea of a lighter listening device." Ibuka had a portable stereo player and a set of standard headphones with him at that time.

Morita instructed his engineers to remove the recording circuit and speakers from the existing taperecorder and put in light headphones.

The engineers got to work, albeit reluctantly. Somehow the idea of a taperecorder without a recording circuit and without speakers did not carry conviction with them. But the idea was honoured and the 'walkman' project was born.

Finally when the 'walkman' was built and sold to global markets, it was an astounding success.

KEY LEARNING

Be liberal in rewards and recognition. A good work that gets recognized gets repeated.

5.9 PASS ON CREDIT

Pass on credit, well in time, whenever deserved. Organizational performance is an outcome of collective effort. Recognize both team and individual contributions.

APPRECIATION

Never hesitate to pass on credit wherever deserved. If required, overdo it. If leadership takes all the credit for itself, for everything that happens in their domain, they sure are laying the doom-path.

Why do people resist appreciating others for the good work, or sharing credit? There could be several reasons like selfishness, jealousy, ego factor, hierarchical compulsion, passive environment, to name a few.

Every organization has a bunch of pessimists who negatively impact the organizational health by negating and discouraging every action, and by looking at every single slippage through huge magnification. They not only detest other people's successes but also relish failures. They love to cause confusion and anxiety and to but in to say, "I told you so". They promote discredit and are a negative influence on performers.

We also come across people with narrow perspectives who tend to devote considerable time and effort in judging and criticizing actions of others. They are heavily into making moral and value judgements. Their approach ranges from being openly critical and demoralising to offering such casual critiques like, "I wouldn't have done it that way".

Individual managements fail to build enjoyable, supportive and sustainable relationships if they believe that they alone were responsible for their personal and professional success. Invariably, it is the right teams and their dynamics that propel this success.

To rightly pass on due credit is like being credible, and is surely an attitude. As managers, we all experience this around us. It is difficult to adequately convey the incredible impact of our positive vibrations toward our employees and business partners.

I recall Keith Harrell who said, "The longer I lived, the more convinced I became that life is 10 per cent of what happens to us and 90 per cent of how we respond to it".

Outstanding performers surround themselves with caring, trustworthy, honest, positive and goal-oriented people, who are motivated, inspired and always itching to perform. They love to take and share credit. Their optimism is contagious and spreads across fast with demonstrated successes.

Understandably, people with judgemental attitudes repel those of optimists with no judgemental values. To them, optimism is the mark of someone who is overconfident, naïve, unrealistic and shallow. However, optimists exhibit the attitude to lead and avoid being stumbling blocks. In my long experience, I have come across several optimists who produced remarkable results with positive attitudes.

Look at Toyota, the company that invented the lean practices, thereby eliminating waste. It focuses on management adding value to the organization by developing both people and business partners. The company encourages the growth of leaders who thoroughly understand their work, live through the company's philosophy, and teach it to others. They also develop exceptional people, and teams who follow the company's philosophy. They also respect their suppliers, challenge and help them to improve.

We all have abilities. All we need is to cultivate and learn how to use them. Senior management should help its employees to learn behaviour-based approaches.

Several top managements display their appreciation of creditable performances by encouraging the performers to be close to them. Unfortunately, this soon leads to unhealthy bias. Other biases include giving preferential treatment to some but not to all staff, rating all staff the same, being overly lenient or overly harsh towards some or all staff and practicing conscious or unconscious local, racial or gender prejudice.

APPLICATION

Cornelius Vanderbilt was a highly successful railroad tycoon in the Unites States of America. He enjoyed frequent travels all across the country, stayed in the most expensive hotels and was extremely choosy in his food habits. He was known as a no-nonsense executive, everything had to be to perfection, and was notorious for his sharp tongue.

In the year 1853, on a business trip, he chose to stay at Moon's Lake House in Saratoga Springs, New York. Immediately after checking in that afternoon, he decided to skip his meal and instead called for a hurried meeting with his senior staff.

It was the job of his secretariat to assemble all the key employees. Several of them were still waiting at the check-in formalities and a few others were planning to move into the restaurant for a relaxed meal.

Finally, when everyone assembled, Cornelius apologised to his colleagues for making them go hungry and ordered some quick food that could be easily served on the discussion table. After looking at the soft potato fries and tasting them, Cornelius got enraged and demanded for the chief chef to personally come over and meet him. George Crum, the head chef of the Moon's Lake House, was immediately summoned. Cornelius insulted George and sent back his fries, demanding that they be cut thinner and fried longer.

In anger, Crum decided to teach the commodore a lesson and shaved off paper-thin slices of potatoes, threw them into a tub of ice water, let them soak, and dropped them into a boiling vat.

Behold! They came out curled crisp and well fried. He then sprinkled salt on them and sent the potatoes back to the Vanderbilt table. Crum was bowled when the guests sent back their compliments and placed several repeat orders.

Soon, "Saratoga Chips" (later to become simply "potato chips") were a featured item on the hotel's menu.

KEY LEARNING

Give credit where it is due, and that too in time.

5.10 ATTEND TO PEOPLE

**Sensitivity to human touch is conspicuous in all leading organizations.
It is the single-most important factor for their success.**

APPRECIATION

Except in outstanding companies, spontaneous employee involvement is rarely visible. Such an involvement has to be evolved, created and institutionalized. In short, it has to be managed.

According to behavioural scientists, today's average employee is producing only 35 to 50 per cent of his or her on-the-job potential. Most of them admit to wasting as much as three hours a day. Managements, therefore, need to attend to people to tap their full potential. There is no single pill to address this need.

What is required is constant attention towards enhanced performances, through proactive, positive and willing efforts so that every employee becomes a healthy worker. Abraham Maslow once stated that "as humans meet 'basic needs', they seek to satisfy successively higher needs and that healthy workers, who are free to think, grow and use information stored in the mind, work harder and smarter".

I have often come across CEOs proclaiming that employees were their biggest asset. Yet, the ground realities were quite contrary. True, they were a great asset, but truly underutilized.

During one of my several interactions with Harsh Goenka, Chairman of RPG Enterprises, in response to his query on how quality management was so successful across the group while I was heading the Corporate Quality function, I confessed that 80 per cent of my time was spent on addressing the needs of my contacts.

During my one-to-one interactions, I constantly urged people to think and talk about the situations that drove their behaviour, both positive and negative. Everyone opened up without hesitation, since they trusted me. Every interaction was a potential opportunity to add value through personal touch.

"Treat others as I would like be treated" was the axiom I followed at RPG.

APPLICATION

Patel was an employee in a pharmaceutical company located in Gujarat, a dry state in India where sale and consumption of alcohol is prohibited, being the birth state of Mahatma Gandhi. However, like in several other government well-intentioned initiatives, there are many loopholes that circumvent prohibition, to the delight of any habitual drinker.

Initially, Patel used to occasionally visit the nearest country liquor bar, along with some select company. Being a bachelor and away from parental control, drinking seemed to relax him and even justify drinking as a social necessity. Soon, the habit controlled him. By 24, he got addicted to the bottle.

After a year or so, Patel got married to a local girl. The marriage was arranged by consent of both the families, who were unaware of his addiction. Even after marriage, he could not give up this habit and continued to regularly visit the country bar. He returned home every night, fully drunk.

Naturally, his work at the plant got affected. His output drastically dropped as compared to his earlier performance. His attendance was irregular, and so became his earnings. Domestic violence dominated domestic peace. Frustration at home was coupled with bouts of helplessness.

Before this bad patch, Patel was an active leader of the Quality Control movement of the company. Some of the circles under his leadership won awards in the local QC circle competitions. He was instrumental in propagating the QC circle philosophy in other companies too, through his hands-on approach. He became an expert in implementing the 5-S methodology aimed at enhanced performances through focussing on cleanliness in the workplace. Unfortunately, all this good work was soon forgotten, and he was an unwelcome member in every improvement team.

The management was quite concerned about Patel. Professional counselling by the company's social worker also did not yield the desired effect, nor did the intervention from his family members.

Then, the company decided to use quality management as a business strategy and embark on structured implementation of Total Quality Management principles across its operations. The strategy was to create total quality culture through implementing quality systems, improving quality practices and developing positive employee responses.

A senior person was appointed to direct the quality movement by driving and facilitating all the employees towards quality. After several interactions, Patel was encouraged to look beyond QC Circles. He was made to understand the importance of a positive attitude and its benefits.

Patel was initially allowed to just sit in the quality improvement meetings, without any compulsion. Gradually he could see the type of enthusiasm the organization had put into place, including rewards and recognitions. More importantly, he could hear more and more team-members telling others how the systematic approach had in fact changed the entire atmosphere at their homes for the better.

One day, not only the quality facilitator, but all members of the improvement teams were pleasantly surprised when Patel stood up and, with an intense emotional outburst, decided not to touch alcohol from then on. More importantly, he promised to behave well with all his family members. Within six months, Patel was back with a bang. He won the Best Team-Member award of the month.

The high point was when, on a pleasant evening, his wife, still a small-built and simple-looking girl, met the quality facilitator and thanked him for being instrumental in transforming her domestic life.

KEY LEARNING

Never neglect the human side of quality.

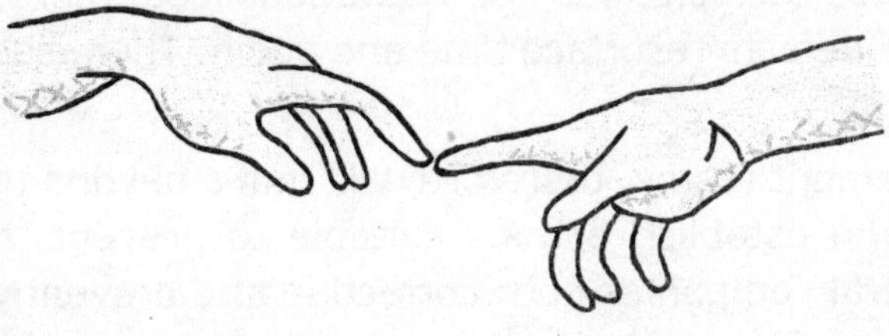

5.11 BE PROACTIVE

All management efforts should be self-driven. Organizations that drive proactively towards improvements are the leaders.

APPRECIATION

Conventional improvement efforts are based on the awareness of the existence of defects that need to be fixed. Corrective steps are taken once defects occur either in the process or in the product. Customers, market and internal feedback drive the organizations to address the defects and take corrective steps to reduce, if not, eliminate them. The corrective steps are always reactive.

Once the defects get corrected, unless the solutions are institutionalized, there is every possibility that the same or similar defects resurface time and again. Then, such corrective actions tend to get on-going.

Experienced and successful improvement teams, therefore, will move beyond the corrective problem-solving approach, and establish actions suitable to prevent the occurrence of the same defects. In several companies both corrective and preventive steps are visible as a matter of routine.

The proactive approach goes well beyond the preventive activity. It doesn't stop with anticipating the likely defects in both processes and products, based on experiences and their analyses. Though preventive quality management is to some extent proactive, it addresses only the likely defects, and hence has limited use to leading companies. The proactive approach looks at all the variables, across all functions that could adversely affect the organizational functioning.

Proactive managements continuously question the current levels of performance, benchmark with the best in the industry in every key operation, and evolve and implement strategies that would sustain their leadership position. They institutionalize continuous improvement processes that have distinct corrective, preventive and proactive approaches.

Most leading Indian companies have by now well drawn-out incremental improvement strategies, initiated mostly when the Indian economy opened up in the early 1990s. While they were helpful in propagating quality culture and focus on customers, employees and suppliers to be competitive, it was only during recent years that these companies began working at breakthrough improvements.

Breakthrough approach aims at remarkable benefits, beyond the established incremental improvements, thereby creating an environment for significant beneficial change — the change as perceived by the customer and as appreciated by the process owners. Organizations that drive such improvements are positioning themselves as leaders and are able to maintain supremacy over the current competition.

APPLICATION

The following abstract of the speech of the President of India Dr. A. P. J. Abdul Kalam at Hyderabad is highly illuminating:

"Why is the media here so negative? Why are we in India so embarrassed to recognize our own strengths and our achievements? We are such a great nation. We have so many amazing success stories but we refuse to acknowledge them. Why?

We are the first in milk production. We are number one in remote sensing satellites. We are the second largest producer of wheat. We are the second largest producer of rice.

Look at Dr. Sudarshan. He has transferred the tribal village into a self-sustaining, self-driving unit. There are millions of such achievements, but our media is only obsessed in the bad news, failures and disasters.

I was in Tel Aviv once and I was reading the Israeli newspaper. It was a day after a lot of attacks and bombardments with deaths. The Hamas had struck. But the front page of the newspaper had the picture of a Jewish gentleman who in five years had transformed his desert into an orchid and a granary. It was this inspiring picture that everyone woke up to. The gory details of killings, bombardments and deaths were inside in the newspaper, buried among other news.

Another question: Why are we, as a nation so obsessed with foreign things? We want foreign TVs, we want foreign shirts. We want foreign technology. Why this obsession with everything imported?

We don't realize that self-respect comes with self-reliance. I was in Hyderabad giving a lecture, when a 14-year-old girl asked me for my autograph. I asked her what her goal in life was. She replied: 'I want to live in a developed India'. For her, you and I will have to build this developed India. You must proclaim, India is not an underdeveloped nation; it is a highly developed nation.

Have you got 10 minutes for your country? If yes, then read; otherwise, the choice is yours.

You say that our government is inefficient.

You say that our laws are too old.

You say that the municipality does not pick up the garbage.

You say that the phones don't work and the railways are a joke.

The airline is the worst in the world, mails never reach their destination.

You say that our country has been fed to the dogs and in the absolute pits.

You say, say and say. What do you do about it?

If you are visiting Singapore, you don't throw cigarette butts on the roads or eat in the stores. You are as proud of their underground links as they are. You honestly pay to drive through Orchard Road. You come back to the parking lot to punch your parking ticket if you have overstayed in a restaurant or a shopping mall irrespective of your status identity.

You wouldn't dare to eat in public during *Ramadan*, in Dubai . You would not dare to go out without your head covered in Jeddah.

You would not dare to bribe an employee of the telephone exchange in London to see to it that your STD and ISD calls are billed to someone else. You would not dare to speed beyond 55 mph (88 km/h) in Washington and then tell the traffic cop, "Don't you know who I am? I am So-and-So's son." You wouldn't chuck an empty coconut shell anywhere other than the garbage pail on the beaches in Australia and New Zealand.

Why don't you spit *paan* on the streets of Tokyo? Why don't you use examination jockeys or buy fake certificates in Boston?

We are still talking of the same "you." You, who can respect and conform to a foreign system in other countries but cannot in your own. You who will throw papers and cigarettes on the road the moment you touch Indian ground. If you can be an involved and appreciative citizen in an alien country, why can't you be the same here in India?

Once in an interview, the famous ex-municipal commissioner of Mumbai, Mr. Tinaikar, had a point to make. "The rich people's dogs are walked on the streets to leave their affluent droppings all over the place," he said. And then the same people turn around to criticize and blame the authorities for inefficiency and dirty pavements. What do they expect the officers to do? Go down with a broom every time their dog feels the pressure in his bowels? In America, every dog owner has to clean up after his pet has done the job. It is the same in Japan.

We go to the polls to choose a government and after that forfeit all responsibility. We sit back wanting to be pampered and expect the government to do everything for us whilst our contribution is totally negative. We expect the government to clean up but we are not going to stop chucking garbage all over the place nor are we going to stop to pick up a stray piece of paper and throw it in the bin. We expect the railways to provide clean bathrooms, but we are not going to learn their proper use.

We want Indian Airlines and Air India to provide the best of food and toiletries but we are not going to stop pilfering at the least opportunity. This applies even to the staff who does not pass on the service to the public. When it comes to burning social issues like those related to women, dowry, girl child and others, we make loud drawing-room protests and continue to do the reverse at home. Our excuse? "It's the whole system which has to change, so what difference will it make if I alone forego my sons' right to a dowry". So who's going to change the system?

What does a system consist of? Very conveniently for us it consists of our neighbours, other households, other cities, other communities and the government. But, definitely not for you and me. When it comes to us actually making a positive contribution to the system, we lock ourselves along with our families into a safe cocoon and look into the distance at countries far away and wait for a Mr. Clean to come along and work miracles for us with a majestic sweep of his hand, or we leave the country and run away.

Like lazy cowards, hounded by our fears, we run to America to bask in their glory and praise their system. When New York becomes insecure, we run to England. When England experiences unemployment, we take the next flight out to the Gulf. When the Gulf is war-struck, we demand to be rescued and brought home by the Indian government. Everybody is out to abuse and rape the country. Nobody thinks of feeding the system. Our conscience is mortgaged to money.

Dear Indians, this article is highly thought-inductive, calls for a great deal of introspection and pricks one's conscience too. I am echoing John F. Kennedy's words to his fellow-Americans to relate to Indians, 'ask what we can do for India, and do what has to be done to make India what America and other Western countries are today'.

"Let's do what India needs from us."

KEY LEARNING

Proactiveness brings out unbelievable results. Reactive approach is just an act of justification.

6 Chapter

LOOK AT PERFORMANCE DYNAMICS

Leading performances are never static. They need to be positioned in a dynamic mode and managed as such.

CONTENTS:

6.1 TAKE INITIATIVE

Ensure that every leadership initiative is relevant and adds value to all stakeholders, both internal and external.

APPRECIATION

Outstanding leaders are at the forefront to initiate developing, facilitating and implementing strategies. They demonstrate unlimited participation and involvement. Even when problems are not escalated to them, they have their own communication channels, keep eyes and ears open, and possess the sixth sense to walk in and initiate accelerated solutions.

Experience tells us that the biggest barrier any leader faces is internal, and not external. There are several attitudinal and psychological barriers, along with a fair dose of scepticism, that need to be overcome.

Every time a new CEO takes over, he or she brings out an individual set of initiatives and encourage employees to work differently on issues such as innovative thoughts, risk-taking, fearlessly owning mistakes and even taking total responsibility to fix problems rather than blaming others. Snobbish CEOs are often replaced by those who want to make work culture fun.

Such initiatives do become a part of the leadership strategy driven from top, the strategy to make its implementation feasible, conspicuous and enjoyable, where everyone follows it willingly.

I personally do not believe that it is so difficult to deal with the top if there is a political climate or immense competition, with very few slots available at top positions. At the same time, I was tremendously benefited by working with top-to-bottom communication channels, since it is always the one at the frontline who has the right information. Except that, as presidents, we have our own ego to satisfy.

I have seen several fast-track men and women, who chose to manage only from the top, after their initiatives were quickly grounded since the lower levels were not taken into confidence. It is a fact that we need these levels to convert these initiatives into reality. Even to dig for information, it is the little chaps who are the best sources. They have the pulse not only on truths and falsehoods, but also on the most devastating half-truths. Having excellent relationships with folks six levels down will ensure total involvement for implementation.

In this information and knowledge era the leaders, while appreciating the power of technology, avoid being over-reliant on it. They know technology by itself is irrelevant and useless if it is not in the care of good hands. They proactively work in that direction.

Corporate CEOs are bright and superb thinkers. They are energetic and all their initiatives are result-oriented. They have the performance of each group company on their fingertips. Though, often, they display a hands-on approach with a personal touch, they create a powerful structure at the corporate headquarters to provide macro-management support. Such a structure is empowered to ensure that constantly upgraded initiatives are continuously flowing from the top that would provide immense value-addition to all the group companies.

Corporate support managements should have wider exposure to enhance the effectiveness of the efforts at company levels. Enhanced results can be achieved only through improved communication, facilitation and handholding. It is essential that such initiatives are constantly upgraded.

Leadership initiatives also include interventions and course corrections in time, to make the companies stay on course. Most failures are not so much due to faulty implementation, but due to delays and bureaucracy muddle. Each corporate support should overcome this negativity, and strive to become a most sought-after resource.

APPLICATION

A petrochemical company in Chennai is a leading producer of the chemical Methyl Ethyl Keytone (MEK), mostly used in the leather industry. Installed in the year 1991, with indigenous equipment and technology, the plant had been focusing on safety from the very first day of its operations. Apart from declaring a highly committed safety policy, the plant management paid attention to every single safety-related measure.

Awareness programmes were conducted on a continuous basis. Employees were made aware of the need for safety and the discipline to strictly follow measures such as wearing safety apparel. Further, to enhance employee appreciation of safe processes, every single process step, both minor and major, was translated into a safety operational step. Employees were made aware of corrective, preventive and proactive steps on safety.

Several measures initiated by the management were conspicuous to everyone who visited the plant operations. When mobile phones made an entry into the country, a warning was sounded against the use of mobile phones near inflammable place such as gas stations, chemical plants and petrochemical units, since the phone rings could be a potential source of generation of sparks. Though there was no concrete evidence to that effect at that moment, such a possibility was brought to the notice of the management.

The management immediately banned the use of mobiles in any of the plant locations. In fact, there was a strict management order to the security to thoroughly check each person entering the plant operations and to ensure that such units are not carried on the person but deposited with the security.

In March 2005, after such proactive initiatives, , the company proudly celebrated successful 4,600 accident free days - a remarkable achievement by any standard.

KEY LEARNING

Create value through dynamic initiatives, as perceived by internal and external customers. Continuously enhance value creation.

6.2 BE OBJECTIVE

Performance at all levels needs to be continuously, objectively, without any bias.

APPRECIATION

An important attribute of a successful management activity is the focus on conspicuous objectivity. Subjective judgements are kept at the barest minimum. Even where gut feels rule, they appear only when decisions are at the final stage and need to be clinched, after looking at facts, data and its analysis with a clear objectivity.

Subjectivity comes into the picture only when the data is sketchy or insufficient or when data analysis is not leading to any meaningful conclusion. In such cases, the objective analysis gets supplemented with subjective opinions. This can lead to managerial decisions of significance without unduly dragging on for a long time.

Objectively assessing any organization or its activities is quite a complex affair. Unlike audits that primarily focus on compliance, assessments look at the whole picture and measure performance against a set of guidelines, without any bias. Assessment is a far more complete process from audit, and has to be necessarily objective based on visible performance. Subjective assessments attract considerable criticism, since they are invariably biased.

Since objectivity is data-based with facts and figures, and is not subjected to personal prejudices, the outcome of any assessment can be easily described and detailed. While appreciating that both the objective and subjective approaches arise along any quality movement, it is desirable to limit the subjectivity factor to the minimum while assessing an organizational performance.

Although each organization is unique, when they are assessed for their levels of excellence, all globally accepted models provide a generic framework that can be applied uniformly to any organization or a component part of an organization. The belief is that organizational excellence is sustainable only through measurable improvements with structured application, with leadership providing the strategic drive.

In such models aiming at structured objective assessments, the objectivity oozes out when one addresses how the organization's leadership is approaching its business objectives, how these initiatives are applied, and the type of results achieved and is achieving on a continuous basis against the best in that class.

During assessments, the companies are evaluated on three dimensions namely: approach, deployment and results. The approach covers appropriateness of the methods employed and their effectiveness, how systematically they are integrated and consistently applied, to what extent the application is based on data and information that is accurate and reliable, use of review cycles, the degree to which the approach is integrated with the normal operations. The approach may also include the evidence of innovation in both management initiative and application criteria.

Deployment refers to the extent to which the applicant's approach is applied to all areas of activity. The factors used to evaluate deployment include demonstrated use of the approach evolved, the extent to which the approach has been implemented to its full potential, and also the appropriate and effective application of the approach.

Results refer to the outcome in achieving the business purposes, and the factors used for such an evaluation are the recorded performance levels, its relative comparisons and benchmarks, sustained improvements and demonstrated high level performance. The excellent results take into account the existence of geometric trends with indication that the negative trends, if any, are well understood and addressed.

Objective assessments help positioning organizations towards world-class quality excellence through several stages, such as, superior quality accomplishment, strong quality implementation and quality awareness from the traditional find-and-fix practices.

APPLICATION

Lala Ramchand's sweet shop occupied the pride of place in the High Street of Rampur town. The enticing display of sweetmeats and other delectables drew crowds of buyers to Lala's shop. A delicious aroma of ghee, sugar, kesar and elaichi wafted out from the kitchen at the back, where culinary experts toiled over the hot fire to produce the sweets that the shop was renowned for.

Ranga was a poor labourer who lived in Rampur. He worked as a coolie for daily wages in the wholesale vegetable market adjacent to the High Street. Everyday he would pass by Lala's shop, and cast a longing glance at the mounds of sweets and the people who were dipping into freshly bought packets of sweets and savouries. Poor Ranga! He would swallow hard, even as he salivated at the sight of those sweets! But none knew better than he that such delicacies were not for the likes of him.

Everyday Ranga's mother packed two dry rotis, along with a green chilli, an onion and a piece of lime. That was his mid-day meal. He and his fellow coolies snatched a few minutes of rest from their hard labour as they ate their lunch.

One afternoon, as Ranga looked for a shady place to sit, he caught sight of a stone bench under a tree just opposite Lala's shop. The bench was usually occupied by shopkeepers or passers-by, but it being 3 o'clock in the afternoon – the siesta hour – the High Street wore a deserted look. Ranga sat on the bench, resting his weary, and opened his lunch packet.

Suddenly, the most delicious smell of spices, flour, potatoes and hot oil wafted in his direction. Of course, it was from Lala Ramchand's kitchen, where preparations were on to stock up on savouries like Samosas and Kachoris for the evening rush that would soon follow. As Ranga breathed deep, his eyes closed in ecstasy, for he could imagine how delicious those eats would be!

Enjoying the mere smell as if he was actually tasting those savouries, which he could never afford, Ranga began to eat his simple lunch. How delicious the dry rotis tasted that day! Finally, he got a heavenly aroma of Burfi and Halwa. Ranga felt he had a square meal, finishing off with a sweet for dessert.

From then on, Ranga decided to eat his lunch at the stone bench everyday. It would be a late lunch, but it was okay because by then, the bench would be vacant, and the delectable smell from Lala Ramchand's kitchen would accompany his workday meal, affording him a pleasure and thrill which did not cost any money!

Lala noticed Ranga on three separate occasions — breathing in those delicious aromas, his eyes closed with a gratified look on his face, as if he had actually eaten a favourite dish. Lala's eyes narrowed in anger. How dare this poor coolie take the smell from his famed kitchen for free?

The next day, as Ranga left the stone bench after his meal, Lala beckoned to him. Ranga was astonished. His eyes widened and his heart raced. Maybe, Lala would give him a few leftovers or broken fragments of the sweets and snacks! Many rich shopkeepers did it, he knew. If that was so, Ranga decided that he would share the bounty with his fellow labourers, and take home some for his old parents. For never in their lifetime could they afford to buy anything from Lala's sweetshop.

He approached Lala who was seated on a comfortable sofa just inside the shop. He could barely take his eyes off the sweets which he was seeing at such close quarters for the very first time!

"So...." drawled Lala,"you are in the habit of sitting outside my shop and enjoying the smell from my kitchen?"

"I.....yes, your honour!" Ranga stammered.

"Out with the money," demanded Lala in a menacing voice.

"Money?" asked Ranga, flabbergasted. "But, why? I haven't taken anything!"

"Oh yes, you have," said Lala sternly. "You poor rogue, even the smell from my shop is not for free! You have been sitting there day-after-day taking in that delicious smell? I have been seeing you enjoying the smell. So pay up now!"

"Is there no justice?" wailed Ranga. "How should anybody be expected to pay just for smelling food?"

A small crowd gathered round the shop as one of Lala's burly servants took hold of Ranga. "Pay up," he demanded menacingly.

"What has the fellow done, Lala?" someone wanted to know. "Has he stolen something from your shop?"

"No, but he has been smelling the vapours that float from my kitchen, and I insist on payment," replied Lala Ramchand.

A holy man who was passing by, heard Lala's reply and stepped forward.

"Here is the money," he said to Lala, holding out a hundred rupee note. "I shall pay for this poor man."

Lala's greedy hand stretched out eagerly to snatch the money. But the holy man teasingly drew it back. As Lala stared, he brought his hand forward, holding the currency note close to Lala's face, waving it right and left.

Lala tried to snatch, but failed. "Give me the money," he demanded hoarsely.

"Give you the money? Oh no!" said the holy man. "This poor man has been smelling your food. You in turn can smell the money as due payment. That is all he owes you!"

The onlookers clapped and cheered as the logic of the holy man's answer appealed to them. "Yes, Yes," they chorused. "He only smelt your food – so you can smell his money!"

Lala Ramchand was non-plussed. Ranga fell at the holy man's feet with tear-filled eyes.

KEY LEARNING

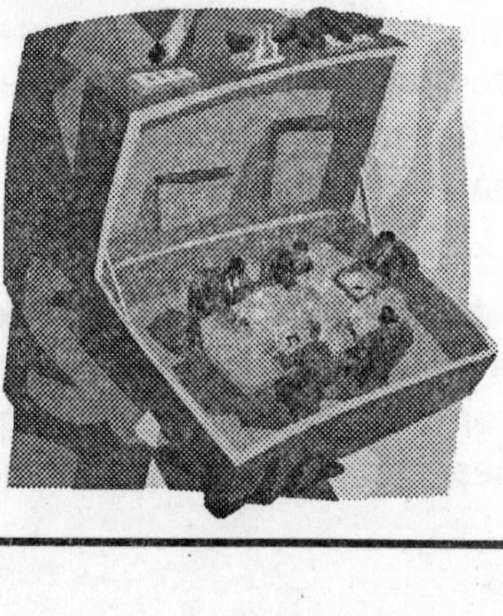

Performances appear powerful only when they are objectively assessed.

6.3 RESPECT EXTERNAL VOICE

Externally driven performances are more effective over the traditional internally targeted ones.

APPRECIATION

Performance improvement efforts, particularly when they are managed internally in the form of Quality Enhancement Teams, QC Circles, Small Group Activities or Kaizen, set targets for the improvement teams which are invariably internal-driven. The quantified improvements are internally discussed and only after identified as achievable, the improvement activity starts. In extreme cases, at the most, they have stretched targets.

One drawback of such an approach is that it neglects competitors' data, benchmarked information and market demands that are invariably dynamically ahead. Only when the targets are externally driven, they throw up vital performance gaps that need to be bridged, even to be in the business. Leading organizations continuously look for this external voice and accordingly drive the improvement efforts.

A recent study indicated that while 80% of the internally-driven improvement teams were successful, the corresponding figure was only 50% when the targets were externally-driven, within the same project duration. The competitive challenge, therefore, is to register high success rates even when targets are based on customer needs and market demands, that too at speeds faster than the nearest competition.

Among the first steps to squarely facing such a challenge is to make customer voices and market needs actionable. It is worthwhile to evolve a Customer Service Programme, CUSP, assign a process owner who collates all the signals emanating from customers, integrate and prioritize them, based on customer-perceived value. Aligning this input, with relevant processes and their capabilities is the next step that needs management attention.

The denominator for capability calculation for each process step is what each internal customer wants and not what the process is designed for. Once that is accomplished, the outcome could be measured in terms of customers' stated and implied needs.

Let's appreciate that each customer is different and communicates differently. He may choose different communication channels and has the sole discretion when, what and how to communicate. Hence, "input from customer" is easier said than done.

In spite of the above limitations, leading companies recognize the importance of the customer and strive to spread it in every function of the organization. They value the frontline employees who have a direct customer-contact, and go that extra mile to create customer-friendliness in them. It is not just the product, nor is it the service that they address, but also the way in which they are delivered. Serving customers, both internal and external, is an obsession throughout these organizations.

APPLICATION

Let me recall the story of Apollo 13 of April 1970:

"Houston, we've had a problem." 55 hours, 54 minutes and 53 seconds into the Apollo 13 mission, this heart-stopping outburst was relayed to mission control in Houston by the astronauts, 3,30,000 kilometres away. It initiated an unbelievable flurry of activity. A coordinated operation to rescue the ailing spacecraft and its jeopardised crew began in earnest.

Having achieved the aim of landing a man on the moon, for NASA, this was considered a 'routine' trip to the moon. And it was, until the oxygen tank number two aboard Apollo 13 exploded during a routine check-up procedure. It was then that technical expertise and divine inspiration worked hand-in-hand to ensure the safe return of the astronauts.

The explosion, which crippled the spacecraft, meant that not only was the moon landing called off, but that emergency measures to bring the craft and crew to earth had to be implemented.

No doubt, all the scientists involved in this great rescue displayed exemplary teamwork and ingenuity. But there was an unseen force aiding their efforts. It was the divine force of prayer. Prayer has often succeeded where other measures seem to fail. In the rescue of Apollo 13, this was also the case.

In an article entitled "What really happened to Apollo 13", Jerry Woodrill, who worked on the mission as the Alarm System Engineer, recognises the prominent and indispensable part prayer played in the successful rescue of Apollo 13. In it, he says, "Many might regard the rescue as the 'spiritualising' of a dramatic event for the sake of religion. I would agree, had I not found much evidence to the contrary."

He adds, "*The New York Times* reported special prayer services. Prayers were said at the Chicago Board of Trade and prayers for the Apollo 13 crew sounded at the Wailing Wall in Jerusalem." Even the United States government realised the necessity of prayer and so Jerry Woodrill writes, "The US Senate adopted a resolution urging prayers."

Finally he writes that his wife has a bracelet and medallion which was "bought at the space centre exchange store shortly after the successful 1970 rescue. The large coin pictured praying hands with the words 'Apollo 13...and the whole world prayed'." This is a clear indication of how much NASA, the people with the most to lose, believed in the important contribution of prayer in their successful rescue.

The entire rescue operation was a perfect example of how effort combined with prayer leads to success.

KEY LEARNING

Everyone who is impacted by your action is your customer. Make serving your customer an obsession.

6.4 BE HUNGRY TO PERFORM

Performances can be deceptive.
Today's outstanding performances can become run-of-the-mill types tomorrow.

APPRECIATION

Everyone tries to perform to the best of his ability. What is best today may not be even acceptable tomorrow. In this dynamically changing world, the level of significance of any performance does drastically change with time. Performances, therefore, need to be continuously reviewed and improved upon.

Can anyone be a perpetual performer? The answer is simply 'no.' Can we at any time say that we are a complete performer? The answer is same, 'no.' Can we at anytime be complacent to feel we have done so much, there is nothing more we need to do for the rest of our lives? Obviously, we would be foolish to think so.

Every performance has a start but has no finishing line. Good performances can be intoxicating while bad ones are demotivating. Outstanding performances are the result of a committed application towards a focussed mission. Everyone can perform, provided one has the passion to do so, and the capacity to doggedly pursue the goal.

A good performer has an insatiable appetite. He has the limitless capacity to seek and grab every opportunity and convert it into an unbound success. If he is already walking, he loves to run; if already running, he loves to race: and if already racing, he loves to be in a marathon. Both his thoughts and actions are boundless.

Outstanding performers are driven by the exceptional blend of emotional involvement and physical activity. They do not understand and appreciate an idle mind, idle thoughts and idle hands. For them work is worship. They drive others while driving themselves.

All powerful leaders have a mind which can think, conceive, modify, meditate, and realise what he desires and what he works for. He appreciates that his organization is only a group of individuals. The organization by itself doesn't think, or act. It has no mind. Only the individual has a mind. He alone can think and act. That is why any organizational thought process is a collection of employees' thoughts. Leaders drive these thoughts and also emotionally get involved.

Lastly, a great leader cares for everyone around as much as he cares for himself, and feeds one and all with as much as he feeds himself. While he has a huge appetite to lead and act, he inspires all others to do so. He enjoys as much when all others perform.

APPLICATION

Are you keen on an organization that has the following achievements?

- Consumes zero per cent fuel
- Uses zero per cent of modern technology
- Has zero per cent financial investment
- Has zero per cent disputes
- Achieved cent per cent customer satisfaction
- Outstanding 99.999999% performance

With an error rate of 1 in 16 million transactions, the performance of this organization is well beyond six sigma.

It is the amazing performance of the Mumbai Dabbawala Association.

Started in 1890, the association was registered as a charitable trust in 1956. Today, with a total employee strength of 5,000, they handle well over 2,00,000 lunch boxes, involving 4,00,000 transactions everyday.

The cost of the service is Rs.300 per month per customer, with a turnover of around Rs.36 crore. Each Dabbawala is a shareholder and earns Rs.5,000 to Rs. 6,000 per month. For their service, as the bonus, they look forward to a month's service charge from the customers, at the time of the Deepavali festival.

The association believes, "Work is worship."

All the members strictly follow the declared discipline that includes no alcohol during business hours, wearing white cap and always carrying identity cards.

Mumbai Tiffin Box Suppliers Association, as it is currently called, has a lean organizational structure, with an Executive Committee of 5 members, who are assisted by Group Leaders heading teams of 20 to 25 Dabbawallahs . The group leader ensures that each individual Dabbawallah collects 35 lunch boxes from homes, deliver them in the offices and return all 35 empty boxes to the homes.

The association was facilitated the world over and won several awards for customer focus. Its performance is a case study at several management institutions in India and abroad. Some of the other achievements are: world record in best time management, entry in Guinness Book of world records, and being registered with Ripley's "Believe it or not."

KEY LEARNING

Never be content with what you achieve. Unlimited improvement opportunities are always awaiting you.

6.5 PAY ATTENTION TO DETAIL

Attention to detail is an act towards perfection. When every single detail is thought about, addressed and executed, it often leads to defect-free outcome.

APPRECIATION

What detail is detailed and when to curtail further detail is a daily challenge to most managements. Conducting of any activity without detailing and due deliberation is discouraged, the only exception being when there is a fire and it needs to be instantly put off. Even here, one needs some detail as to what is to be used to effectively extinguish the fire and how.

Whether it is a manufacturing set up or a service organization, the frontline functions should be aware of every single detail that would positively, and also adversely, impact the performance. As we move upwards on the hierarchical ladder, decisions are not so much based on the nuts-and-bolts of the detail, but on an analysis of the available details. While executive summaries have little impact on operating customer-interface levels, presentation of extensive data is not greatly relevant to the top management.

A simple rule is detail only to the extent that you feel helpful. Do not encourage the collection and analysis of plenty of data, since such an analysis often leads to paralysis. Planning for detail is also essential so that what is collected is accurate, measurable and traceable. An easy and effective way of collecting data is through well-designed formatting.

I have found the Data Sheet an extremely easy and helpful tool for data collection. It also helps to kick-off any management effort towards defect-free performance. Designing a Data Sheet is very simple and follows a few logical steps. The items to be checked are pre-printed so that recording against each item becomes easy. Further, when the data is recorded in a specially designated form, often it can be interpreted directly from the sheet itself.

Data Sheets can provide details on every single organizational activity, including design, production, maintenance, process control, sales, marketing, finance and also product and service quality. They are, thus, helpful to providing quality data of not only the final assembly or operation but also to carry out a comprehensive check of quality that has been built through the previous stages.

Most improvement teams prepare a checklist prior to initiating any activity and check for its exhaustiveness. Then, every single identified detail is addressed and noted for its compliance. Deficiencies, if any, are thrown up as deviations and are corrected then and there, while further analysis helps preventing recurrence of such defects.

Collection of false data, the data that is not consistent with facts, poor methods of data collection, wrong transcriptions of data, wrong calculations, abnormal values, lack of attention to data robustness and finally wrong method of application are some of the pitfalls that are scrupulously addressed to ensure that the data and information is effective.

A common pitfall in the preparation of a Data Sheet is its lack of exhaustiveness. There is a tendency to evolve such a list casually, without any seriousness, and cover only the most 'visible' items and not the important ones. Often, such a list may cover only those items which are considered important by the managers, and not fully satisfying the needs of its customers, both internal and external. Such pitfalls can be overcome only by addressing every singly detail, however, minor or trivial, and then prioritizing them based on their importance.

APPLICATION

Let me recall the story of six men born blind and living in the same locality. They meet every evening at a huge parade ground and discussed the events of the day. Being physically challenged, each one had something to share that would lift the spirits of others. Like any other employed, they too had their own concerns with their bosses and their weird ways, and loved to share with other friends, often with a liberal sprinkling of some salt-and-pepper.

One evening, while they were discussing, an elephant was guided into the ground and the kids around made a lot of commotion.

When told about the entry of an elephant, the blind friends began discussing among themselves about how the elephant looked. In office, when they were busy with their work, all they heard was that an elephant was a big animal.

"How big and what was an elephant like?" they wondered.

They were embarrassed to ask such a question to the people assembled, particularly the boys. They decided, instead, to walk up to the elephant and feel it for themselves. They touched the elephant at different parts and exclaimed occasionally!

The First Man: "The elephant is like a wall."

The Second Man: "The elephant is like a spear."

The Third Man: "The elephant is like a snake."

The Fourth Man: "The elephant is like a tree."

The Fifth Man: "The elephant is like a fan."

The Sixth Man: "The elephant is like a rope."

Each of these descriptions was distinctly different, with nothing in common. All six men repeatedly talked of the same description. After a while, they started arguing for long and disputing loud.

The fact was, all the six men were right in part, but were wrong about the full picture.

KEY LEARNING

Attention to detail is a discipline. This needs to be cultivated and ensured in every walk of life and at each step.

7 Chapter

BE COMMITTED TO OUTPERFORM

Commitment to outperform is contagious.
It recognizes no barriers.

CONTENTS:

7.1 FIRE IN THE BELLY

Spread success stories like wild fire.
Success breeds success.

APPRECIATION

Well-promoted success stories kindle enthusiasm and encourage excellent performances. All extraordinary performers are inspired and fired with a desire to achieve something new, and something out of this world.

Path-breaking inventions and discoveries are products of inspiration. As a material scientist, I believe that nature is endowed with several useful materials that are being discovered over centuries. It is the urge to use them for the benefit of mankind that is resulting in several inventions. Metal nails were invented by the ancient Egyptians to join coffins. The later inventions like wheel, gear, silk and cotton yarn, and many other items are by now so much a part of our life, they are taken for granted.

With globalization and a fast-paced life, the current-day inventors are firing their imagination so wild that industry leaders eagerly inspire and drive competence among them. The level of inspiration is proving boundless. Commercialization of any new development is an instantaneous logical step, with fierce market competition driving its acceleration.

Though the magnifying and reflective qualities of glass was discovered well over 2000 years ago, their remarkable application in the camera technology, during the past decade, was mind-boggling, aided by the design and development of integrated circuits. The same is true of the Information Technology industry. In a short span of 30 years, computers have shrunk from room-sized models to ones that can easily fit into the palm, with everincreasing operating speeds and memories. During the 1940s, scientists invented the microwave ovens to cook food faster by using radio waves, and by the

1950s, the first microwave ovens were being sold. Industry leaders contributed a lot to this technology explosion.

Current inventors have so much fire in their minds, thoughts and actions, every new development is pushing out, by several miles, the boundaries of human knowledge. Surely, knowledge explosion is inspiring one and all. While not all can be inventors, everyone is promoting inventive minds.

Expansive managements have expansive thoughts. The inspired among them invariably magnify their thinking patterns. They think and dream with creativity. They have a bloated vision. For them, action is a habit. They have tremendous tenacity, and have an unlimited drive within themselves to doggedly pursue things. They don't presume it may not work. Instead, for them it would always work.

When you believe, your mind finds ways to succeed. Any difficult encounter becomes unsolvable only when you think it is unsolvable. Solutions with several alternates become visible by believing that solutions are possible. The more the solutions, the greater the inspiration.

Believing that we have the capacity to do it is powerful and unshakable. Companies like General Electric, who use the slogan, "Progress is our most important product" always offers something new, every time and all the time. They love to be creative. They appreciate that not all creative thoughts lead to inventions and discoveries. Creative thinking which simply finds new, improved ways to do things also gets total encouragement.

Unlike the inventors engrossed in basic research, many successful thinkers are conscious of their environment, manage the surroundings and recondition themselves towards success through action-orientation and by being doers. They are always positive, forward-looking, optimistic, love to seize an initiative and be a crusader to break barriers. They undoubtedly are role-models, love to systematize their achievements, and create islands of excellence. They get led to lead. Such persons become invaluable resources in spreading an exemplary performance enhancement culture.

APPLICATION

The statue of liberty in the harbour of New York is a great symbol of man's dedication. cooperation, hardwork, determination and achievement.

During the second half of the 1800s, the people of France decided to gift a unique statue to the people of the USA, in recognition of the friendship established during the American Revolution, and engaged the renowned sculptor, Bartholdi to work on a masterpiece. Bartholdi began construction of the 47 metre high statue in France, in 1875, planning to complete it by the year 1876, to commemorate the centennial of the American Declaration of Independence.

The statue was to be a joint effort between America and France and it was agreed upon that the Americans would build the pedestal, and the French the statue and its assembly in the United States. However, both the countries had a lack of funds. In France, public fees, various forms of entertainment, and a lottery were among the methods used to raise funds, while in the United States, benefit theatrical events, art exhibitions, auctions and prize fights helped.

Meanwhile in France, Bartholdi required the assistance of an engineer to address structural issues associated with designing such as the colossal copper sculpture. Alexandre Gustave Eiffel (designer of the Eiffel Tower) was commissioned to design the massive structure.

Back in America, fundraising for the pedestal was happening particularly slowly, so Joseph Pulitzer (noted for the Pulitzer Prize) opened up the editorial pages of his newspaper, "The World" to support the fund raising effort. Pulitzer used his newspaper to criticize both the rich who had failed to finance the pedestal construction and the middle class who were content to rely upon the wealthy to provide the funds. Pulitzer's campaign of harsh criticism was successful in motivating the people of America to donate. Financing for the pedestal was completed in August 1885, and pedestal construction was finished in April of 1886.

The statue was built in France and was transported to New York in July 1884. The facts below show how much effort, dedication and cooperation went into this landmark work:

- Weight of copper used in the Statue: 81,300 kg
- Weight of steel used in the Statue: 1,13,400 kg
- Total weight of the Statue: 225 tons
- Height from base to torch: 46.84 metres
- Thickness of copper sheeting: 2.37 mm

The statue was dismantled into 350 individual pieces and shipped in 214 crates. It arrived in the New York harbour in June 1885. The statue was assembled on the pedestal in four months time. On October 28, 1886, the dedication of the Statue of Liberty took place in front of thousands of spectators. She was a centennial gift, ten years late.

Eleven years were required for the total completion of this monumental Statue of Liberty, USA's National Monument, who officially celebrated her 100th birthday on October 28, 1986. To day, the welcoming Statue of Liberty inspires the world.

KEY LEARNING

There is no backseat while managing for excellent results. Once achieved, provide the widest possible publicity to all inspired performances.

7.2 DETERMINE TO EXCEL

A commitment to succeed needs will and tenacity. Excellence is a product of determination.

APPRECIATION

Organizations shine when everyone is committed to succeed. The success is not based on a singular effect but is a result of the combination of several activities, carefully formulated, well-knit and structured for implementation.

Excellent performances are never products of an accident. They are well thought about and well executed. They not only call for clarity in what is to be achieved but also demand meticulous approach to succeed in reaching set objectives.

Improvement processes in such organizations are invariably well institutionalized and internalized with no ambiguity on what is to be achieved. Everyone aligns himself to the common goals and works towards achieving the same. Targets set in such cases are not just figures of convenience, but are evolved based on careful consideration, such as comparatives with competitors, market demands and benchmarks.

Leading performers do recognize that while achievement against targets is necessary, it is often not sufficient. What is required is steadfast determination to excel, even under severely adverse conditions. This calls for facing challenges boldly, and converting adversities into grabbed opportunities.

It is imperative today for managers and executives of all organizations to know how to manage in these ruthlessly competing times. They should not only effectively manage today, but address the emerging challenges of tomorrow. Outstanding performers love to take up challenges. They task to manage what there is and work to create the necessary environment to succeed in the future. They also periodically upgrade themselves to hold on to the leadership, so that they are always ahead of competition.

Organizational leadership is a matter of quality commitment, awareness of core strengths, focusing on these strengths and riding on them. It is imperative for all businesses to know their strengths, and base their strategies on them. Some basic questions they don't hesitate to ponder over are:

What is it that our customers believe that we do well?

What are the areas in which we consistently perform?

Which of our well-demonstrated strengths are unique?

What are our specific strengths that are highly visible?

Do they continue to be the right strengths?

Are they the strengths that fit into the opportunities of tomorrow?

Are they the strengths that can face the challenges of tomorrow?

Are we adequately deploying our strengths where opportunities exist?

Have we institutionalized dynamic gap analyses?

What additional strengths do we have to acquire?

How are we going to acquire them?

While seeking the right answers for the above questions, every attempt is made to objectively present information about failures and ensure that shortcomings are not clouded but presented as a factual case study. Any disregard to such a discipline negates organizational commitment and determination to excel. As Aristotle said, "Excellence is not an act, but a habit."

APPLICATION

With America's striking in 2003, Iraq's infrastructure was destroyed, including its electric power supply. Transmission towers were uprooted and structures distorted. There was total darkness in many localities and the population was starving for lack of basic necessities, like drinking water. Both the urban and the rural population were adversely impacted. The local population was getting restless. It became imperative to the occupying American forces that they need to start rebuilding the nation in the shortest possible time.

Against the global tender floated by Iraq authorities with America's help, KEC International, a leading Indian transmission tower-maker desired to respond with its quote to rebuild their electric transmission system. As the largest tower-maker in the country, with a global presence, it was somewhat easy for the company to appreciate the technical requirements of the enquiry.

However, Iraq's needs were highly demanding even during such adverse conditions. They wanted KEC to take the total responsibility of rectifying the damaged towers, designing, fabricating and supplying new ones where needed, commissioning them, and finally coordinating with the local authorities to demonstrate transmission of the required load to the local population. Such a comprehensive requirement also demanded a war-footing activity under adverse conditions.

The company had to overcome several obstacles, the most testing one being the presence of company's personnel in the midst of deafening war sounds and frightening war effects. To be in tune with the country's culture, adjusting to the local climate, overcoming language barrier, distasteful culinary habits—some of the KEC officers were strict vegetarians—a hungry, frustrating, angry, poor and lawless local population were some other challenges. The greatest challenge was to complete the work within three months of acceptance of the order, amidst such adversity.

One of the early responses of the company was that, though it appeared to be a hugely profitable job, the risk involved was too high, with Iraqi authorities refusing to take any responsibility for the safety of the personnel working at the field. Moreover, they had set an unreasonable timeframe for the job. But a section of the senior management agreed that despite the high risk, the job should be taken as a challenge.

KEC's management committee decided to move ahead. Once the order was received, the tower design time was shrunk by 90 per cent. The supply-chain management was on cent per cent top gear. Procurement of over 9,000 tonnes of steel sections was shortened by 80 per cent. All critical suppliers were motivated to perform within stringent timeframes. Fabrication was done on warfooting. Towers in loose condition were dispatched well in time and every batch was well escorted up to the site.

Obtaining travel authorization and addressing the highest safety concerns of KEC officers were the biggest challenges for the HR management, with no responsible government system in place in Iraq. However, these were appropriately addressed, along with issues such as local travel across war-torn Iraq. Simultaneously, tremendous efforts were put in to mobilize local resources for downloading at the site, reassembly and erection of the material despatched from India. Logistics were considered in advance and implemented with local authorities, even under difficult conditions.

It was a great experience for all those involved in this mission. When the towers were finally erected and electricity restored in time, everyone was moved by an elderly lady who walked up to the team of achievers with tearful eyes and embraced each one of them. An outstanding example of excellent performance achieved through grit and determination.

KEY LEARNING

Commitment to succeed is not adequate. Many professionals exhibit this attribute, but the leaders demonstrate the determination to excel.

7.3 HAVE A PASSION TO SHINE

Be passionate to perform. Passion should ooze out from every activity of the management.

APPRECIATION

A number of competences are conspicuous among leading performers, providing them with a powerful framework for achieving operational excellence. Depending upon the level of their achievement, organizational functions can be positioned at one or more of these ladder-steps propelling them towards sustained leadership.

The very first step is Quality Awareness: Awareness that quality is well above the traditional find-and-fix; awareness that quality of the deliverable is as dictated by the customer; awareness that quality of the deliverable is built in the operating system, not in inspection of products and services.

With the presence of such awareness, organizations begin to address all processes, systems, delivery, documentation and, in fact every single commitment to stakeholders, as a part of managing for quality. More importantly, quality management begins to focus on the management of poor quality cost as an imperative, with the belief that higher the quality lower is the cost, and it is only when the product or service has additional features, it costs more. Not because it works better.

Moreover, customer expectations being dynamic, there is no finishing line for quality. This awareness, when spread across all operations, encourages continuous improvement – an important facet of quality management – through judicious application of various tools and techniques.

The second step is Quality Attitude, when positive attitudes towards managing quality are well appreciated and applied. Quality Attitudes are often cultivated through the application of the right improvement modules and are promoted through "training for quality" in addition to "training for skills." The inputs that could result in positive attitudes are instilled by the top management, with value statements like vision and mission providing the drive. During this step, employees voluntarily and proudly participate in team-building exercises and demonstrate communication skills, presentation skills and positive behaviour patterns.

The positive attitudes lead to Quality Commitment. Those standing on and operating from this third step are highly visible with employees believing that quality is manageable through quantification and, like any other management discipline, can be managed as an important component of business strategy. They begin enjoying success stories and learn to consistently compete for leadership position, irrespective of the size of their operations. The degree of commitment varies from one organization to the other, and depends on the extent to which an organization has attempted to be a leader, through the management of quality, by simultaneously working on recognizing and rewarding quality performers.

High levels of commitment are often measurable and demonstratable. Commitment is visible in all activities –including those interfacing with internal and external customers. All the employees will then get self-driven proactively and ensure excellent performance in processes, systems and deliverables.

Those who are committed to quality performance are determined to ensure the same, even when they encounter the most difficult obstacles. Quality Determination, as the next step, leads organizations to stick on to the set course, and avoid the temptation of taking convenient shortcuts. They don't encourage cutting-the-corners, but squarely face the road blocks right ahead. The determination to succeed itself succeeds when it is supplemented with hardwork. Everyone who is determined works hard to reach the goal. Even the smartest manager works hard to reach his destination. Every top Indian performing executive, without exception, burns the late night oil.

Those who are determined to consistently perform are supported by great abilities and the right attitudes. With so many positive qualities springing out of the determined executives, the outstanding individuals and their establishments demonstrate how passionate they are towards unmatched performances. Quality Passion is built into their activities and operations, and gets ingrained and infused. The passion to shine through excellent performances in processes, systems and deliverables becomes a routine.

APPLICATION

The story of Dr. R. K. Sampat is a case of demonstrated passion towards quality performance.

Way back in the year 1972, when our son Vamsi was of two years, we had a chance meeting with Sampat. One of our old Punjabi neighbours was at our house one afternoon and saw Vamsi, very weak, clutching to his mother and crying continuously. He had reason to do so since almost two months before he had severe diarrhoea.

In his case, the diarrhoea bouts were intermittent. The first time he had the problem, our family physician prescribed him the usual medication. With this allopathic treatment, Vamsi recovered quickly, only for it to recur immediately after. Though he was born a chubby boy, he now turned pale and got increasingly weaker.

Each time we took him to the doctor, he was dispensed the same medicine, except in increasing dosage, potency or both. However, nothing helped and the dosage was too much for the boy. The after-effects became obvious. Vamsi just could not cope with the medicines.

One evening, he suddenly showed signs of extreme dehydration. He was referred to a child specialist, who wanted the boy immediately brought to his consulting clinic. It was 11 in the night when Vamsi was rushed to the hospital for glucose. After two days in the hospital bed, he returned home with a battery of medicines prescribed by the specialist doctor. But, they worked only for a week or so.

The problem recurred with vengeance. He continued to throw out whatever was fed to him. It was at that time this pious Punjabi lady visited our home. As providence would have it, her daughter too had undergone a similar experience when someone suggested she shift from allopathic medicine to homoeopathy under Dr. Sampat, who later cured this girl.

We met Dr. Sampat who was over eighty, and had long years of established practice of homoeopathic medicine. His treatment was so effective, everyone believed he had the Midas's touch. His expositions on homoeopathy were legendary. He had a roaring practice built over four decades and established himself as an incredibly eminent doctor.

During later years, Dr. Sampat's passion overtook his initial desire of being in the rat-race of the medical fraternity. Dr. Sampat felt all his thoughts, actions and resultant successes were driven by the Almighty, and the only way he could give back to him was to show concern to the society and the needy. He moved out from his posh consulting room to a simply done-up facility of 10 square metres and relocated himself to a community hall, to be easily accessible.

While hearing Vamsi's case history, Dr. Sampat's queries were specific and to the point. Within 20 minutes, he fully grasped the case, and obviously confidently assured us that the boy would soon be cured. He got up from his seat, made a small mix of powders himself in our presence, gave half of it to the boy, and asked us to administer the balance the same night. He asked us to bring the boy again the next evening. When we enquired his fee, he smiled and said 25. Presuming that meant 25 rupees, I removed the notes from my pocket when, with a hearty laugh, he chided that possibly I was used to spending thousands of rupees on doctors. He took just 25 paise!!

When we took the boy the next evening, Dr. Sampat observed that there was a remarkable improvement, and that the boy was responding to the medication. He repeated the dose, took another 25 paise as his fee, prescribed the medicine and said that we need not visit him again – which we never had to.

What an outstanding case of competence to passion!

KEY LEARNING

Be passionate while preaching and practising high performance management.

7.4 CONSTANTLY INNOVATE

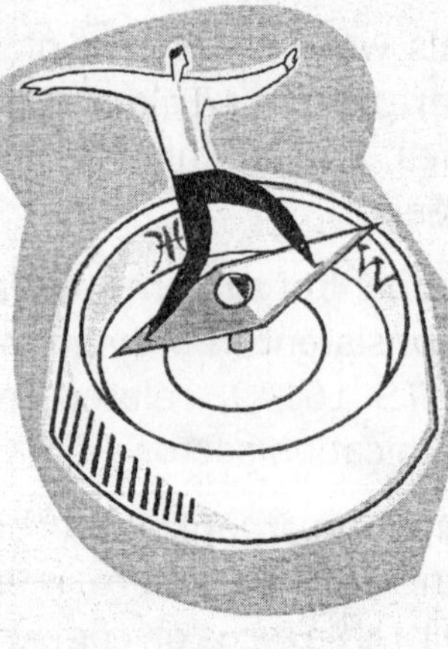

Nothing is constant in life, except birth and death. Only innovative thoughts and actions can manage change towards leadership.

APPRECIATION

While inventions are products of human desire to create something new, innovation strives to create something better. Both address facing the challenges of global dynamics.

If we look at the past and integrate with the current and crystal ball the future, quality management seems to be moving along five major phases.

The first one was when outstanding one-off pieces were created as breathtaking beauties such as Ajanta and Ellora, Taj Mahal, Kutab Minar and even the Iron Pillar at Delhi. When these were created by the artisans, their only aim was to bring out monuments of exquisite beauty. There was obviously no limitation on any of the resources, nor was time for completion a constraint. Every one apparently worked with total devotion, passion to perform and obviously with tremendous pride to excel.

The second phase was during the industrial revolution of the early 1940s, with quantity focus, addressing quality through inspection, testing, sampling, Statistical Quality Control (SQC) and Statistical Process Control (SPC). Product and process inspection came into prominence during this period. Quality was the prime responsibility of the quality control departments. Organizations took pride in stating that they had a very large workforce manning their quality control departments. The bigger the quality inspection at the finished product end, the greater was the quality organization.

Obviously, ensuring product quality to the required standards was left to QC department, with greater focus on product inspection and clearance for dispatch to customers.

The third phase was during the early 1970s when the Japanese successfully brought about the concept of Total Quality Management. Soon it was established as a powerful tool for enhancing organizational competitiveness, and moving towards organizational excellence through operational improvements. A number of Quality Gurus made significant and outstanding contributions towards propagating the TQM movement.

Consequently, several continuous improvement models were developed globally and got popular worldwide. Some of the well known ones are: Juran's Trilogy, Croby's Zero Defects, Quality Circles, Kaizen, Small Group Activities, Management by Policy, Quality Function Deployment and Business Process Reengineering.

Focus on quality systems got a fillip through the development of system standards, such as ISO 9000, ISO 14000 and ISO 18000, aiming at consistent improvements in performance, along with industry specific standards like TS 16149, related to the automobile sector and TL 9000 corresponding to the communication sector.

The fourth phase is that of the 1990s when fiercely competing organizations began realizing the inadequacy of continuous improvements of an incremental nature, more so since such improvements are almost always internal-driven, with little focus on competition and customer's dynamically changing expectations. While appreciating that the continuous improvements encouraged quality culture, leading companies began encouraging breakthrough improvement methodologies like Six Sigma and Total Productive Maintenance.

The fifth one is the currently emerging phase through the realization that the current formulas and techniques are already proving to be ineffective. New models need to be developed to take head-on the challenges posed by issues such as knowledge explosion, speed of technological advances, management of change, creativity and innovation, transformation, and adaptability to a flat world. Today's competitive, connected and complex world is surely demanding this evolution.

APPLICATION

I recently read, with considerable interest, USA's Global Exploration Strategy, focusing on two overreaching issues: why the country is returning to the moon and what its scientists and engineers plan to do when they get there. The strategy includes a comprehensive set of the reasons for embarking upon a human and robotic exploration of the moon and creating settlements in space. What had prompted them to unfold such a strategy?

We all admire the way the world is continuing to move forward, sharply focusing on the manned space programme: to go out beyond earth orbit for purposes of human exploration and scientific discovery.

The launching of several successful unmanned space vehicles originated when the global scientific and technical communities made their first successful move on 4 October 1957, when the Soviet Union launched Sputnik, the first ever artificial satellite, into orbit.

By 12th April, 1961, within a three-and-half-year timeframe, technology had advanced so fast that Yuri Gagarin could be put into orbit, sustained there, and safely brought back to earth. And on 20th July, 1969, two men, Neil Armstrong and Edwin Aldrin became the first people ever to set foot on any celestial body other than the earth. From sputnik to the moonwalk, it took less than twelve years.

This "great leap for mankind" as Armstrong called it, was a triumph of almost unimaginably complex technologies, innovatively refined to the demands of space exploration. A powerful booster rocket had to be developed; the astronauts were required to master all the subtleties of space navigation; they needed the protection of an infallible life-support system, and a moon-lander that could never be tested on earth, yet must never fail in space.

It would be misleading to talk as if the technologists behind the space effort simply saw a complex of problems and set about solving them: if that had been the case, moon-landing wouldn't have happened so quickly. For a couple of decades at least, they have also been trying to devise a motor car that doesn't pollute the atmosphere, to control and harness nuclear fission, and to devise an economical supersonic aircraft.

Technological innovations are not made simply because some momentum of history makes them inevitable, but because scientists and engineers direct their efforts to make these specific developments happen.

Even as children, we were fascinated with looking at the moon, stars and the galaxy. We heard beautiful poems about the legendary old lady sitting pretty on the moon and responding to our wishes. The ancient Greeks made gods out of the moon and stars, romantics choose them as their symbol of eternal love, astrologers use them to predict the future, and writers fantasized about the existence of alien creatures dwelling in other worlds. It is only in the last century, with the enthusiasm for space exploration growing ably supported by innovative theorists and engineers, that the technology of space exploration was fast unfolding.

Skylabs, unmanned repair stations and reusable rockets are no more futuristic developments. It seems very likely that the developments of the next twenty-five years will be even more astonishing than the past, with the likes of International Space Stations, considered as the most complex construction feats ever undertaken.

Using the space station and building an outpost on the moon to prepare for the trip to Mars are among the critical milestones in the fascinating journey for space exploration.

KEY LEARNING

Discourage any statement that management's success is based on nationality, religion, nature and size of business.

7.5 CRITICALLY ASSESS

Assess the outcome of management initiatives and their deployment. Aim for excellence.

APPRECIATION

I had an amazing meeting the other day with a dynamic, young, thirty-year-old Indian CEO, owning a highly successful technology company. Floated by him and two of his friends about 5 years before, the company's annual billing galloped from rupees one crore to well over rupees 100 crore during this period. During our meeting, he also unfolded tremendous growth plans. The promoters' primary business focus was on designing, developing and maintaining customer-centric technology solutions through high quality deliveries.

At the end of the 30-minute intimate interaction, I asked him what he was looking from a management consultant like me, when the going was so good. He said that while he had a steep climb, he could slide down much faster if his processes were not scientifically measured through designed assessments. He believed that his company would score not over 40 out of 100 and would be nowhere near the best industry benchmark. He was keen to, therefore, quickly evolve a suitable Operational Excellence model, specifically in line with his visionary objectives, and introduce dynamic performance assessments.

Most organizations are accustomed to audits. Quite often they are mandatory; such as financial audits or management audits. Audits are performed to verify, by examination and evaluation, whether certain applicable elements of performance have been effectively implemented in accordance with specific requirements. Audits are also helpful in detecting problems or deficiencies before the conditions deteriorate.

Assessments, on the other hand, highlight how effectively the leadership is directing the company's long-and short-term objectives, how effectively processes are being managed and how effectively the employees are focussing on their customers, both internal and external. They provide objective information that enables the management to make sound decisions, with greater clarity. Assessments also help in monitoring and identifying the quality of relationships between people, processes and products. More importantly, they accelerate organizational drive towards excellence.

Assessments are also aimed at evaluating the importance and value of each management initiative and its effective deployment. In fact, their exhaustiveness can be stretched to several areas that may be considered trivial, and do not get normally noticed. Similarly, assessments can be drilled down to levels well below the comfort zones of the management process. Thus, outstanding assessments can be both exhaustive and educative.

Leading companies demonstrate the usefulness of critically assessing every single activity relevant to the broad parameters of leadership, application and results. The criteria associated with these three parameters are, by now, well documented globally in several quality excellence models. These models are providing a framework to evolve, measure and improve every process step and strive to achieve benchmarked results of performance.

All assessments are based on the guidelines developed to assess each of the criteria and are positively oriented, with both strengths and areas for improvements sharply determined, unlike audits that aim primarily at finding faults. At the end of each assessment, the organization is provided with a valuable feedback report that proves to be a tremendous value addition.

APPLICATION

On Monday, December 18, 2006, the Pentagon mentioned in its quarterly progress reports on the Iraqi war, mandated by the Congress, that the enemy achieved a strategic success by unleashing a spiral of sectarian killings by Sunni and Shiite death squads that threatened Iraq's political institutions. The Pentagon described Iraq as a nation moving towards a civil war, with violence at record highs of 959 attacks per week, declining public confidence in the government and little progress toward political reconciliation.

The attack levels in Iraq hit record highs in all categories nationwide, as the number of the US and coalition casualties surged 32 per cent from mid-August to mid-November, compared to those of the previous three months. During the same period, the number of weekly attacks rose 22 per cent, from 784 to 959. In January 2006, the ethno-sectarian executions were 180 which rose to 1,028 by October, while ethno-sectarian incidents rose from 63 to 996 during the same period.

This was in spite of the presence of well over 1,40,000 US forces and a growing contingent of Iraqi security forces, projected to be 3,25,000, both trained and equipped.

But, the number of soldiers and police actually present for duty was far lower than the number trained and equipped. At any moment only 2,80,000 were "available" on duty, and about 30 per cent of that number was "on leave", leaving fewer than 1,96,000 on the job. The Pentagon document conceded that the major US and Iraqi military operations, during the last quarter, could not quell sectarian violence in Baghdad.

In spite of this ground reality, President Bush insisted that the violence in Iraq was not a civil war. But almost everyone, including Colin Powell, former Secretary of State said that United States was losing what the later described as "civil war" in Iraq. While President Bush considered a "surge" of 15,000 to 30,000 personnel added to that force, there was a growing opinion that the US military should move away from insurgency to focus mainly on hunting Al-Qaida terrorists, as proposed by the top military leaders.

Bob Woodward, in his outstanding book on the plan of attack on Iraq provides details on the intelligence assessments of Iraq's alleged weapons of mass destructions. The book is a definite account of how and why President George W. Bush, his council and allies had tutored their assessments by twisting the then prevailing ground realities in order to justify his attack on Iraq. The book beautifully brings out the graphic details of behind-the-scenes manoeuvrings towards this most controversial war.

The mid-term "thumping" the GOP suffered on November 7, 2006 was largely a repudiation of the increasingly unpopular war in Iraq, a conflict linked to neo-conservative ideology, lead by Defence Secretary, Donald Rumsfeld. It was on March 19, 2003 that President Bush ordered the start of war on Iraq. It was on March 21 the so-called "shock and awe" air war began.

After September 11, 2001 Bush decided to circumvent the United Nations and declare war on Iraq. The principle pretext was that Baghdad was supposedly stockpiling weapons of mass destruction. From the get-go, the Iraq war was a matter of choice. Like a "high-stakes poker player pushing in all his chips in one hand, Bush bet the credibility of the United States on the notion Sunnis and Shiites wanted democracy. When Bush declared 'Mission Accomplished', he was totally exposed with his phoney pretext for war, namely WMD and All-Qaida operatives in Baghdad."

According to Woodward, "The decision-making leading to the Iraq war – concentrated in sixteen months from November 2001 to March 2003 – is probably the best window into understanding who George W. Bush is, how he operates and what he cares about." Obviously Bush did too much, attacking the wrong country at the wrong time for the wrong reasons.

Bush conceded, for the first time, on December 19 "we're not winning (the war), we're not losing" in an interview with *Washington Post*. He said that he still wanted to expand the overall size of the "stressed" the US armed forces to meet the challenges of a long-term global struggle against terrorists. This assessment was a striking reversal for a president who, days before the November elections declared, "Absolutely, we're winning."

The Congress approved $500 billion so far for terrorism-related operations, including Iraq and Afghanistan. An additional $100 billion is in the pipeline, and the overall expenditure of $600 billion far exceeds what was spent on the Vietnam war. The end of the tunnel is yet alluding the disgraced current USA administration.

KEY LEARNING

Assessments are not for fault-finding. Nor are they products of fanciful actions. They add value to management efforts.

7.6 INSTITUTIONALIZE BREAKTHROUGHS

All continuous process improvements need to be institutionalized. It not only ensures their sustenance but also provides the foundation as stepping stones for breakthroughs.

APPRECIATION

Management approaches leading to performance excellence are not standalones but are an integral part of organizational activity. They are to be implemented with a focus on achieving sharply defined objectives on one side and looking beyond on the other. Though each approach may be managed independently and reviewed against its objectives, both these approaches are synergized through networking for maximum benefits.

Facilitators develop expertise in one or more of these approaches. The expertise is conspicuous and aims to ensure definite success in meeting the current and visionary objectives. We should recognize that it is individual employees who drive and implement performance management. It is personality-based during the initial periods of the improvement journey, but it gets irreversible when such an activity is institutionalized and individual bias is avoided. The same is true for breakthrough improvements.

When the product and service performances are improved with improvements in the process quality, it is advisable to quickly institutionalize every single improved process. Unless this is done, the organization may not only find it difficult to retain the benefits but also lose the momentum for improvement leadership.

One method by which the quality improvement activity is institutionalized is to incorporate the improvements through system documentation like ISO 9000 standards. This will surely ensure system quality leading to consistency in performance. However, it should be recognized that attention to compliance to minimum levels of documented systems is necessary, but is not sufficient to bring about radical changes that could transform any organization as a benchmarkable one.

For leading companies, continuous improvement is a routine. They go well beyond and look for breakthroughs. As Juran said, any breakthrough is an organized creation of a significant beneficial change; change as perceived by customers as beneficial. It is only the breakthroughs that ensure organizations sustain their leadership positions..

Breakthrough improvements are neither incidental nor accidental. The most successful among them are built over a solid foundation of the culture of continuous incremental improvements. Experience shows that breakthrough culture is sustainable only when an organization has established quality culture and when incremental improvements have become its routine.

The principle benefit of the breakthrough culture is confidence–building that anything can be dramatically improved. While continuous improvements ask 'why' while considering alternatives, the breakthrough approach asks 'why not?'.

Breakthrough teams always look beyond. They depend a lot on deeper insights and newer ideas. They look for quantum leaps. They constantly seek new ideas and approaches and enjoy opening up new opportunities to think, act and improve. They love to be path-breaking and like to see their ideas mould into concepts and then onto realities. They aim at quantum leaps in performances and are not content with marginal benefits.

The breakthrough approach helps in thinking out of the box. Through persistence, it encourages the ability to break old paradigms, move on to creative ideas and successfully implement them.

APPLICATION

During the past four-decade association with several organizations and individuals, I always kept my ears and eyes open to continually learn from them, particularly the outstanding performers.

Each time I met and interacted with such persons, I have been enamoured and got inspired to perform better. I am convinced that there is no finishing line for excellent performances. The more we achieve, the more we wish to.

When I was recently in San Jose, California, USA I had a memorable evening with Dr. Stephen W. Hawking, the renowned cosmologist. He spoke for an hour on the "Origin of the Universe" and it left everyone spellbound.

Hawking is perhaps the most recognized and celebrated scientist of the last thirty years. He is best known for his work on developing the theory of black holes and the structure of space-time. With his work, cosmology is making a paradigm shift in thinking about the formation of stars, galaxies, black holes and, indeed, about the origin of the universe itself.

Hawking was born on 8th January, 1942 in Oxford, England. Since1962, Hawking had suffered from a wasting disease called motor neuron disease. By the early 1970s,

Hawking was weighing not over 100 pounds, permanently confined to a wheelchair, unable to walk and barely able to talk. His induction into the Royal Society in 1974 was a stunning triumph for a man who, a decade earlier, thought he would not live to his twenty-fifth birthday. In 1978, he received the Albert Einstein award, considered the highest honour in theoretical physics.

Dr. Hawking suffers gradual disintegration of the nerve cells in his spinal cord and brain that regulate voluntary muscular activity. "He has overcome this crippling disease to become the supernova of world physics. He is leaping beyond relativity, beyond quantum mechanics, beyond the big bang, to the 'dance of geometry' that created the universe."

He discovered that stars are exploding two, three, and sometimes four times in the first minutes following the initial explosion. Further, a newborn black hole is a chaotic object, and this chaos seems to be what drives creation.

Hawking is blessed with a prodigious memory. His colleagues are constantly stunned by what Hawking has remembered. He could dictate, from memory, forty pages of equations.

He communicates from his wheelchair with a computer system run on batteries under the wheelchair. He builds up sentences by running a programme called Equaliser, and once he builds up a sentence, he sends it to a Speech Synthesizer. He, thus, gives lectures, write papers, writes equations in words, with computer programmes translating into symbols. Currently, he has a universally programmable infra-red remote control, attached directly to his computer system.

Hawking says, "I don't have time to do the things I can do, so it doesn't seem important to worry about the things I can't do." On his 65th birthday, in January 2007, the celebrated physicist was planning a flight into space, and did it on April 26 when he experienced weight loss by flying up to 24,000 feet over the Atlantic, off Florida, in a modified jet which carried him, a few of his physicians and nurses, and dozens of others. He, no doubt, inspires one and all.

Hawking's November 6, 2005 speech was illuminating and truly inspiring. What he continues to demonstrate is beyond the comprehension of any common man. His achievements against several odds are unparalleled.

His work showed, "we are just an advanced breed of monkeys on a minor planet of a very average star. But we can understand the universe. That makes us something very special".

KEY LEARNING

Breakthrough is an organized creation of a significant change, as perceived by customers.

7.7 STRETCH THE STRETCH

All performances are elastic. They can be stretched only to stretch further.

APPRECIATION

Life is a limitless effort and performance is a limitless result. The process of learning has no boundaries. It is seamless and all pervading.

We humans are distinguished by our brain. We have the ability to think, to reason, to judge, to visualise, to create and to appreciate. Every second, the brain sends and receives some fifty million messages, though we don't capture all of them. It controls our thoughts and emotions, stores our memories, and directs every voluntary and involuntary action of ours.

Inside the brain are some 1,00,000 million cells, and from each one comes a baffling maze of perhaps another 1,00,000 fibres, all of which are active whether we are awake or asleep. To my mind, the best description for stretch-to-stretch is the human brain. What we effectively use at anytime is a tiny fraction of the brain's potential.

As a child, primitive reflex actions like firm holding of our parents' fingers or any object placed in the hand are developed. Within two months, the grip is strong enough for the child to lift himself.

During the later periods of childhood, the term usually applied to the phase of human development between infancy and adulthood, every single action such as crawling, sitting, walking or running is a performing art. They are held and guided, during this period, with stretched hands. Their performances grow under protective umbrellas. Even then, every moment is a challenge, and every minute is an effort.

Life experiences and expectations pose enough challenges during early adulthood, and during this period, one's performance reflects the prevalent intimacy, compassion, love and care. Adolescents, although regarded as naïve and inexperienced, quickly develop the values required for dealing with others. Relationships with their parents, colleagues, peers and older adults undergo changes. They begin to understand their roles and how they relate to one another.

The late adulthood to early 40s pose further challenges. It is often characterized by settling down in life. People strive to increase the financial and emotional investments they make. They'd often become more focused on advancing their careers and gaining stability in their personal lives. Most performances peak during this period. The human qualities show up and work in progression. They start valuing others through the realization they are not standalone performers and try adapting to the circumstances. The human brain reaches the highest efficiency during this period, though, even here, only a miniscule capacity is put to effective utilization.

From then on, it is downhill, physiologically speaking. It was reported that, compared to when you were an adolescent, you are three times as likely at age 50 to have chronic sinus problems, thirteen times as likely to have arthritis or high blood pressure, seven times as likely to have an orthopaedic impairment. Visual impairment is five times as common, hearing impairment is almost nine times as prevalent.

True leaders never lose their self-esteem in this difficult and challenging journey of life. They simply adapt to the unfolding changes with grace and continue to move forward. They recognise that management would get more and more challenging and emerge successful by supplementing through psychological management. They continue to be at work pursuing their dreams and never missing even a single little window of opportunity.

The newborn's learning process begins with birth and, given the right environment and stimulus learning, becomes as natural as breathing. Milestones reached by most children, like recognition, turning, crawling, speaking and walking, are the same. They reach these milestones with unfailing regularity. It has always amazed me that while most children are equally learned during childhood, why don't all of them achieve similar results as adults? Why do most lag behind while only a few surge ahead? The only plausible explanation seems to be the "Stretch" factor. The desire to stretch beyond others. The desire to stretch beyond oneself. This desire to excel is what motivates each one of our super achievers and distinguishes them from the others.

APPLICATION

Albert Einstein once said, "there are only two ways to live your life: one is as if everything is a miracle, the other is as though nothing is a miracle".

Despite his image as the supreme absentminded professor, with tousled hair, Einstein had a great deal to offer anyone who seeks to awaken the body and soul and link experience together. Einstein was inspired by the quest for pure truth and beauty.

We do share with Einstein an interest in how we learn and what we can do with that knowledge. For all the sophistication of his intellectual constructs, a look into the workings of his mind reveals that Einstein is the perfect guide to some of the least sophisticated power that we all have, the childlike sense of play and humour that is the essence of his genius.

Born in Ulm, Germany in March 14, 1879, the young Albert Einstein was a dreamy, curious individualist. As a child, "he was fascinated by wheels and all other objects with moving parts." At the age of five, he was fascinated by the compass presented by his father. He developed interest in music when his mother presented him with a violin. His uncle Jacob encouraged his search for truth by supporting his love of mathematics, giving him books on Geometry and Algebra.

Einstein's emphasis on the role of visual learning process is legendary. He was a creative dreamer. He often said, "A normal adult never stops to think about problems of space and time". He made history through his stretched thoughts.

One day while still in his early teens, Einstein went for a walk on a grassy hillside. He closed his eyes, enjoying the warmth of the sun, and imagined that he was riding on a sunbeam out into the universe. In his mind's eye, he travelled into eternity and was shocked to discover himself returning to the place from which he began. If you travel forever in one direction and return to the place where you began, what does that tell you about the universe? Obviously, it must be "curved".

As a result of this and other imagination games, Einstein intuited his path-breaking theory of relativity.

"Humour and humility are expressions of the brain's ability to make connections." Einstein had them in abundance. Before his theory of relativity was confirmed, he said, "if relativity is proved right, the Germans will call me German, the Swiss will call me a Swiss citizen, and the French will call me a great scientist. If relativity is proved wrong, the French will call me a Swiss, the Swiss will call me a German, and the Germans will call me a Jew".

Einstein knew how much he did not know. "As a human being, one has been endowed with just enough intelligence to be able to see clearly how utterly inadequate that intelligence is when confronted with what exists," he wrote to the queen of Belgium. "If such humility could be conveyed to everybody, the world of human activities could be more appealing."

There is no better example than Einstein for Stretching the Stretch. Finally, are you more likely to get your breakthrough ideas while daydreaming resting in bed, driving in your car, or taking a shower rather than when you are at work? If you answered yes to any of these questions, you may be surprised that you are already thinking like Albert Einstein.

KEY LEARNING

Performances can be stretched as far as we desire.

REFERENCES

1. Michael, Hammer, and James, Champy, "Reengineering the Corporation", 1993, Harper Business, New York.
2. Detective Shadow, "Tricky Mind Trap Puzzles", 2000, Sterling Publishing Co., Inc., New York.
3. Suzanne Bates, "Speak Like a CEO," The McGraw-Hill Companies, 2005.
4. Michael J. Gelb, "Discover Your Genius," Harper Collins Publishers, New York, 2002.
5. Peter F. Drucker, "Innovation and Entrepreneurship: Principles and Practices", Affiliated East-West Press, New Delhi, 1986.
6. Kaoru Ishikawa, "What is Total Quality Control?" Prentice-Hall Inc., N.J., 1985.
7. Gerald Nadler and Shozo Hibino, "Breakthrough Thinking", Prima Publishing & Communications, CA, 1990.
8. Jack Welch, "Straight from the Gut"', Warner Books, New York, 2001.
9. HDH Pramukh Swami Maharaj, "Turning Point", 2004, Swaminarayan Aksharpith, Amdavad.
10. Tony Osman, "Space History", St. Martin's Press, New York, 1983.
11. Philip B. Crosby, "Completeness", Penguin Group, New York, 1992.
12. Bob Woodward, "Plan of Attack", 2004, Simon and Schuster, New York.
13. David Hoffman, "Who Knew?" 2000, MJF Books, New York.
14. Fr. C. P. Varkey, S. J. "If He and She Can...", 2004, Better Yourself Books, Mumbai.
15. Donald T. Phillips, "Lincoln on Leadership", 1992, Warner Books, New York.
16. Vaswani J. P., "You Can Make a Difference", 2006, Sterling Paperbacks, New Delhi.
17. Cathy Lowne, "Speeches that Changed the World", 2005, Bounty Books, London.
18. Christopher Meyer, "Fast Cycle Time", 1993, The Free Press, New York.
19. Alan Axelrod, "When the Buck Stops with You", 1952, Penguin Books, New York.
20. A. P. J. Abdul Kalam, "Ignited Minds", 2003, Penguin Books, New Delhi, India.
21. Jeffrey A. Krames, "The Welsh Way", 2002, Tata McGraw-Hill, New Delhi, India.
22. Richard T. Pascale, "Managing on the Edge", 1990, Simon and Schuster Inc., New York.
23. Joan E. Kremer, "Successful Managers Handbook", 2000, Personnel Decisions International, Minnesota.
24. Phil Clements, "Be Positive", 2004, Kogan Page, New Delhi.
25. Stephen P. Robbins, "Truth About Managing People", 2002, Pearson Publication Inc., Delhi.
26. Thomas L. Friedman, "The World is Flat", 2005, Penguin Books, London, England.
27. Edavana Damodaran, "Human Destiny", 2003, Sahayog Publications, Mumbai, India.
28. Keith Harrell, "Attitude is Everything", 2005, Harper Business, New York, USA.